How to Win

the Sale

and

Keep the Customer

How to Win
the Sale
and
Keep the Customer

Telephone Sales Scripts, Marketing Letters, Voice Mail & Email Messages

Ann Barr

To order additional copies of this book, contact:
Xlibris Corporation
1-888-795-4274
www.Xlibris.com
Orders@Xlibris.com
18820

Contents

INTRODUCTION

Did you know that you could dramatically increase your sales just by changing a few words in your sales presentation?

During my first year in telephone sales, calling new prospects was something I dreaded. Until I discovered how to change the way I felt about cold calling and how to change the words I used during the call. First, I realized that the way prospects responded to my calls was—for the most part—up to me. I found that when I came to the office in a terrific, cheerful mood—feeling great and full of energy—the prospects I called were receptive and even friendly. On the other hand, on rainy Mondays . . . or Tuesdays or any other day, if I felt tired or not enthusiastic about calling, the prospects I called sounded unreceptive and unfriendly.

Then, an amazing thing happened. I put two and two together and realized it was up to *me* how my prospects responded to my voice, my words and my attitude on the telephone! This opened the door for some tremendous sales. And I want to share the magic formula with you.

Key Point: This is crucial: *You* must believe you have great products and/or services for your prospects and customers. Why? Because the first person who needs to be sold on the value of what you are offering is you. Because your attitude will shine through—in your phone calls and your letters. Your prospects will hear it in your voice and read it in your words. When you sound excited and happy, it will be contagious. It will transfer to your prospects (unless you are calling a really grouchy, negative person who wouldn't sound happy even if s/he won the lottery.)

"The greatest discovery of my generation is that a human being can alter his life by altering his attitude."
—William James (1842-1910)

Word Power

The true currency of business today is words. Communicating your ideas, the features and benefits of your product—using words to achieve your goals is the single most important activity of any business. Look at the scripts, letters, voice mail and E-mail messages in this book and personalize them to fit you and your own personality. When you are positive, confident and comfortable, it will come across to your prospects.

I wish you success and good selling!

Ann Barr

CHAPTER ONE

How to Make Cold Calling Easier

Pave the Way for Your Call

Cold-calling is probably the most dreaded activity in a sales person's day. The reason? Nobody likes to be rejected. Fear of cold-calling has ended thousands of sales careers. How can you make cold calling easier and reduce the fear of rejection? By advance planning.

Send an Introductory Letter First

Spending five minutes and the cost of a postage stamp can make cold-calling more comfortable for you. Sending an introductory letter ahead of time to a specific person in the company you plan to call, will pave the way for your cold call. If the letter is well written on your business stationary, you will set yourself apart as a professional. If possible, include a colorful savings coupon.

Your cold call will then be a follow-up call. **If you intend to call 50 people each day, send 50 personalized letters each day.** Personalized meaning "Dear [*prospect's name*]."

Write a note on your calendar to call these 50 accounts on a specific day—5 to 8 business days after you mail the letters. You can say—after introducing yourself and your company—to your prospect:

"I have a note on my calendar to call you today." And then: "I'm calling to follow up on the letter we mailed to you last week with the *[insert $$ amount]* savings coupon good through *[insert coupon expiration date]*."

Building Trust

The fact that you are following up on a letter gives you a legitimate reason to make the call. And even though it is a *cold call* (meaning you are calling a new prospect), you will have more to talk about during this initial call.

The first telephone call can begin a trust-building process—and the first step of a business relationship. People will buy from someone they trust.

Remember this: Marketing studies show **it takes seven contacts within 18 months to get a new sale.** These contacts can consist of phone calls, letters and/or postcards in addition to other forms of marketing which require permission in advance—namely, fax marketing and e-mails. Don't be discouraged if the prospect does not buy from you during the first phone call. If they have a need for your products or services, follow up on a consistent basis with letters, postcards and telephone calls.

How to Get Less Rejection

One of the major problems faced by telephone sales reps is how to make cold calls with less rejection and more success. Marketing research has found that **your success rate will soar** when cold calls are preceded by a well-written introductory letter on business letterhead. Why?

If the letter is written well, on attractive business letterhead stationary, **you will be perceived as a professional**—someone who has taken the time to carefully compose a letter to introduce himself or herself before calling.

What should you write in your introductory letter? Introduce yourself, your company and the products you sell—and especially the benefits the prospect will get when s/he buys from your company. Written benefits will answer the prospect's questions as s/he reads your letter, and **the most important question your prospect asks is: "What's in it for me?"**

There are four key points to remember when writing introductory letters:

1: *Always* include the contact name—for the person you are writing to—in the letter and on the envelope, otherwise your letter will end up in the trash and you will have wasted time and money.

2: *Short paragraphs* are easiest to read and the letter should be no longer than one page.

3: *Don't mail out too many letters at one time.* If you intend to make 50 telephone calls a day, mail 50 letters each day. Don't mail out 500 or 1,000 letters at once. *Reason*: By the time you call the 500th or 1000th person, s/he will have forgotten about your letter.

4: *You will create more interest* if you include a "limited time—special offer" in your letter. For example: A monthly special "good through September 30th" or whatever month you choose to mail your letters. An offer available only for a limited time will often prompt the prospect to call *you*. Repeat the offer in a P.S. to get the prospect's attention. Most people read the P.S. before they read the body of the letter. Enclose a flyer on brightly colored paper to increase your success rate.

Calling a New Prospect

Your first call is the first step in building a relationship. It is rare that a new prospect will buy from you on the first call. Think of this call as the first of at least five calls you will make to this prospect, so don't offer to send them everything at once. In other words, the first material you can send is your company information, then the second time you call, you can send something else, like a Customer Care or Information Package. After the third call, you can send them your monthly sale flyer. After the fourth call: A new product announcement.

Research from *Sales & Marketing Executives International* indicates that **81% of all sales made are made in the fifth call or later in the sales process.**

Cold Call Example
Get the Name of the Decision Maker

Example of the first call to a new prospect:

Sales Rep: "Good morning, this is [*your first and last name*] calling from [*your company name*] in [*city or town where your company is located*]. Could you tell me the name of the person who orders [*your products*] for your office?"

(This is instead of asking to speak to the person. You need the name for your records and for future calls.)

Another way to get the name of the decision maker:

Sales Rep "Good morning, this is [*your first and last name*] calling from [*your company name*] in [*city or town where your company is located*]. We are sending out new updated product information to [*name of their company*]. Who should that be addressed to?"

Introductory Letter

Date

Name
Title
Company
Address

Dear [*name of prospect*]:

Enclosed you will find a savings coupon worth $10.00 on your first order of widgets. The coupon is good through the end of this month on any size order you wish to place. This is our way of inviting you to take advantage of the products we offer.

Our Widget Department now stocks a variety of new products and we have enclosed a brochure for your convenience in ordering.

I will be calling you within the next few days to follow up and let you know how we can provide you with several new time-saving programs.

Sincerely,

[*your name*]
[*your title*]

Enclosure: Savings Coupon and
Company Brochure

Introductory Letter
From new sales representative

Date

Name
Title
Company
Address

Dear [*name of prospect*]:

The purpose of this letter is to introduce myself to you. My name is [*your name*] and I am your new [*your title*] for [*your company*].

You are a valued customer and we appreciate your business. It is exciting to be here in the [*insert name of department*] and to be able to work with you.

I will be calling you within the next few weeks to let you know about the new cost-savings products now available. If you need anything, please do not hesitate to call—we have a terrific [*insert product or service*] sale going on now.

I look forward to working with you. If there is anything you need, or if there is any way we can improve our product offering or our service to you, please let me know.

Sincerely,

[*your name*]
[*your title*]

Introductory Letter
Introducing new department

Date

Name
Title
Company
Address

Dear [name]:

Thank you for your recent purchase from [your company]. You are a valued customer and we appreciate your business.

Today I'm writing to introduce you to our new [department]. We stock most branded and generic [products you sell] and offer next-day delivery on in-stock items. Our pricing is competitive and we've built our [years in business] reputation on providing excellent service to our customers.

As your [title] I can assist you with any [products you sell] questions you may have.

In a few days, I will call to tell you about an exciting new product we are offering to our preferred customers!

Sincerely,

[your name]
[your title]

Introductory Letter
With attention-getter

Date

Name
Title
Company
Address

Dear [*name of prospect*]:

Congratulations on reaching your 25th year in business. What a milestone! Although I've seen your name in industry publications, I realize we've never had the opportunity to talk.

The purpose of this letter is to introduce myself and let you know in advance that I'll be calling you next week to give you an overview of how our new [*Department*] can meet your [*Products/ services*] needs. Enclosed is our company brochure with my business card.

I look forward to talking with you next week and setting up a time to meet.

Sincerely,

[*your name*]
[*your title*]

Introductory Letter

Date

Name
Title
Company
Address

Dear [*name of prospect*]:

I'm writing to introduce myself to you. My name is [*your name*] and I work for [*your company*] here in [*your city or province*].

We stock over [*number of products stocked by your company*] different [*type of products*] locally. You can get next-day delivery on in-stock items and our staff has been trained in [*type of products you sell*] needs with over [*number of years experience*] years experience. Please feel free to call us with any questions you have about [*products you sell*]. If we don't know the answer, we will find it for you.

Our prices are extremely competitive—sometimes lower than large warehouse pricing. And we carry both branded and generic [*products you sell*].

Enclosed is our newest price list for your [*type of products*]. In a few days I will follow up and call you. Please feel free to call me if you have any questions. With [*your company name*] you get quality products, excellent service and a knowledgeable staff.

And you don't even need to stand in line!

Sincerely,

[*your name*]
[*your title*]

Enclosures

<<>>

Re-Introductory Letter to current customer

[*Date*]

Name
Title
Company
Address

Dear [*name of prospect*]:

Over the past few years you have been using Ace Widget Company as a supplier. As the Account Representative for A.W.C., I want to tell you that I appreciate your use of us as a supplier and I value your business.

Many new items have been added to the inventory here at Ace Widget, so I am enclosing a list of the different brands of products that are currently available. If the items are in stock, delivery will be within 48 hours. If the products are to be specially ordered, delivery will be within five to seven days.

The enclosed catalog lists retail pricing. Please call for quantity pricing and availability. I am available here from 8:30 a.m. to 5:30 p.m., Monday through Friday at (757) 555-8000, extension 237.

All prices quoted include delivery and terms are net 30.

I'll call you next week to answer any questions you may have about our products.

Sincerely,

[*your name*]
[*your title*]

Enclosure: Widget Catalog
with retail pricing

<<>>

Introductory Letter
Requesting an appointment

Date

Name
Company
Address
City, State, Zip

Dear [*name of prospect*]:

I know you want to stay informed about developments that relate to your job, your business, and your industry. That's why I'm writing to share some exciting news.

I believe you'll be interested in a recent announcement from [*your company*]. We are offering a new solution, specifically developed to help organizations like yours deal with the challenges of [*procuring type of products/services you offer*]. Our new [*your new department*] offers [*features, advantages, benefits your department offers*].

If you agree that this is something that could benefit [*prospect's company*], I would like to talk with you about it at your convenience. Would [*date you plan to visit*] work for you? I'll call to confirm the appointment or to schedule one more convenient for you.

It's exciting for us at [*your company*] to be able to offer leading edge solutions, and it's a great opportunity for you to [*obtain the benefits your department provides*]. I look forward to talking with you soon.

Sincerely,

[*Your name*]
[*Your title*]

<<>>

Action Plan

Which part of this chapter will be most useful to you?

_____

_____

_____

_____

How will you use these ideas?

_____

_____

_____

_____

On what date will you begin using the ideas?

_____

CHAPTER TWO

Opening Statements

The Key to Successful Calls

What you say in your introductory statement on the telephone is critical. Your opening statement is the central element in your sales call and you only have nine to fifteen seconds to get the prospect's attention. During these first few seconds of the call, your prospect has three immediate mental questions:

- ▸▸ "Who is this person?"
- ▸▸ "Why is s/he calling?"
- ▸▸ "Why should I listen?"—or: "Will I gain anything from listening?"

Without an opening statement that arouses the curiosity and attention of the listener, nothing else matters. If the prospect has done business in the past with you or your company, make that connection during your opening statement. This will immediately get the listener's attention.

If you are making a cold call where there is no past connection, your opening statement is even more critical. You need to know in advance what type of business you are calling. If you are calling an accounting firm, for example, and you have other accounting firms as customers, use this as the opening statement. "We specialize in supplying local accounting firms with [*insert your products or service*]."

The point you need to communicate in the first few seconds is "We have a product or service that may help you and I need to learn more about you to find out." The key is in using the right words. Before the call, answer these questions:

▸ What do prospects want most as it relates to my product/service?
▸ What do they want to avoid?
▸ How can I help them do their job more effectively?

When you answer these questions, you have the basis for your opening statement—something that will cause the listener to become curious and want to take the time to speak with you.

Why 9 out of 10 Cold Calls Fail

Why do nine out of ten cold calls end up without success? The same reason that 98 out of 100 sales letters end up in the trash can.

Questions

How do you feel when a telemarketer calls you at home while you're having dinner? What are you thinking? Most likely you're wondering who this person is, wondering why s/he is calling you and asking the mental question: will I benefit from listening?

When *you* make a sales call, your prospect is thinking all of the same thoughts.

The Connection

In the first nine to fifteen seconds of a sales call, either you answer the prospect's mental questions or s/he won't want to continue listening to you. Either an *immediate* connection is made or the prospect decides it's not worth her time to listen. In the first paragraph of a sales letter, either an *immediate* connection is made or the prospect stops reading the letter.

Is it All About You?

If the first 9 to 15 seconds is used to talk about **you** or your company, or what **you** want to sell, the prospect will not be interested. But if that valuable time is used to make a connection and let the prospect know how s/he will benefit, studies have found that your chances to make a sale increase by more than 50%.

The opening statement must convey the impression that you have a product that will help them and you need to learn more about their needs.

Setting Objectives

Before you make your calls, have at least three objectives in mind—write them down in advance. Two reasons: (1.) You shouldn't start off on a journey until you know where you're going and (2.) if you don't succeed in your first objective, you have other objectives you can accomplish. You won't feel you've failed if you can achieve at least one of your objectives. So, what could your objectives be?

1. To make a sale
2. To get the decision-maker's name
3. Find out which products or services they buy
4. Find out how much and how often they buy
5. Find out who they buy from
6. Find out what price they pay
7. Find out how they feel about their current vendor or service provider
8. Get the name of another buyer within the company.

9. Make an appointment for a follow-up call.
10. Make an appointment for an in-person visit
11. Get a commitment that they will read the catalog brochure or price list you send to them.

The *Mental Block*

Have you ever been in the middle of a sales call and suddenly had a *mental block*? Or you were making a sales presentation and stumbled over your words? If this has happened to you, you are not alone.

It has happened to nearly everyone. You are finally talking to that prospect you wanted to reach. And now that you have him on the telephone, you are at a loss for words. You begin your sales presentation and suddenly you have a mental block—you can't think of what to say next. Why does this happen? For several reasons. Among them:

Reason #1. You are new at the job and haven't had much experience, or—

Reason # 2. The customer called when you were in the middle of doing something else. You weren't prepared for the call. Or—

Reason # 3. You call a customer and s/he asks you a question which takes the conversation in a different direction.

Reason # 4. You have made the call without setting and *writing down* your objectives for the call.

Preparing for a Mental Block

Reason # 1. If you are new at the job and haven't had much experience, ask for help from your supervisor or manager. Don't be afraid to ask—no one is born knowing how to say the right words to prospects and customers.

Reason # 2. If a customer calls when you are in the middle of doing something else, be honest and tell the customer you need a minute to look at his file. If this is a new prospect and you don't have a file on this account, ask questions to find out what his/her needs are—and learn why s/he is calling you.

Examples

- "Thank you for calling. How can I help you?"—or:
- "I'm glad to hear from you. What prompted your call today?"

  Let the CUSTOMER do most of the talking, so you can find out as much as possible about what prompted his/her call and then you will learn how your products/services can help.

Reason # 3—You call a prospect and s/he asks you a question that takes the conversation in another direction.

To prepare for this situation, WRITE DOWN—before you call the prospect—your objectives for the call and the questions you intend to ask and the information you want to give the prospect. When your objectives and questions are written down in front of you, you can always refer to them if the conversation takes a turn in another direction.

Reason # 4. You have made the call without setting and writing down your objectives for the call.

What Results do You Want?

Before you make each call, decide what you want to accomplish. Decide what you want to happen as a result of this call. Examples:

1. **You would like further information that will help you to qualify the prospect.** Information that will tell you whether or not your products/services can fill a need the prospect has. To accomplish this objective, write down—before you call the prospect—the questions you need to ask. If your questions are written where you can see them during the call, you can refer to them if the conversation takes a turn in another direction.

   Or—

2. **You want the prospect to read the information you have sent to him/her.** To accomplish this goal, ask questions that will get a commitment from the prospect. Example: "By when will you have looked at our catalog?—I'll make a note to call you on that date." Or: "Let's set a date for our next conversation. I can call you back on Thursday afternoon. Okay?"

Getting Past the Gate Keeper

The screener. The gate keeper. Those words strike fear in the heart of anyone who has ever made a cold call. Strike out with this person and you're a goner.

She (sometimes he) is usually efficient and organized. Her/ his job is to keep people away from the boss—people the boss doesn't want to—or doesn't have time to—talk to. Often that means you—the sales person.

The screener is not always treated with respect by callers. Especially callers who become annoyed when they are not immediately put through to the boss. What does not treating the screener with respect do? Annoys and irritates this employee. Is this person important to you? Most assuredly *yes*. S/he can make your job easier or shut you out of the company you are trying to get into.

First Step

Your job will be more difficult if you don't have the name of the decision maker (DM). Call first (before you intend to talk with the DM) and ask for the name because you are "updating your files" or "sending information." After you have the name, wait a few days before calling back. If you are unsuccessful at getting the name of the DM this way, there are other ways to find out.

1. Look through the prospect's web site. Often you will find several different contact names you can use.
2. Call the company and ask to be put through to the sales department. Sales reps are usually willing to help other sales people—and will often give you the name of the decision maker you are looking for.

Questions to Ask the Screener

It's amazing what happens with the right words and a respectful tone of voice. Here are a few tips:

▶ "Can you help me out?"
▶ "Can you point me in the right direction?"
▶ "I'd like to be of some help to your company. Could you

tell me who I would talk with to introduce the benefits of [*insert your product or service.*]"

▶ If the screener is not sure who the decision maker is (for your particular product or service) and puts you through to someone's assistant or secretary, it's very important not to assume that person is *not* a decision maker. One way to ask the question is:

> "Are you the person who makes the decision regarding your [product/service] needs, or do you have someone who does that for you?"

Everyone likes to feel important and if you can convey an attitude of respect to the screener or the assistant to the boss, you may make a friend who can help you get to the decision maker.

Now that you have written your introductory letter and gotten past the screener, what do you say when you talk to the decision maker?

Let's work on creating your own unique *attention-getting* opening statement!

Prepare for Each Telephone Call

▶ Clear your mind of everything else.

▶ Erase the last call from your mind.

▶ Clear your desk of everything except what you will need for your call—product information, catalogs, price lists, pen and paper to make notes.

▶ Write your opening statement. You will feel comfortable and sound more professional if your opening statement is prepared in advance. Rehearse it with a friend or use a tape recorder.

▶ Write down your objectives for the call.

▶ Take notes. Jot down everything your prospect tells you.

This will help when handling objections and your notes will help you when making follow-up calls.

Greeting Checklist

1. Your name and the prospect's name
2. Your company name
3. Connection/Attention-Getter
4. Reason for the call
5. Benefit statement
6. Question relating to a need

Example—Calling a Current Customer
Selling office equipment supplies

(1.) Good morning Mr. Jones, this is Mary Smith from

(2.) ABC Office Equipment in Sacramento.

(3.) Your Hewlett-Packard printers are under maintenance with our company.

(4.) The reason I'm calling today is: The Hewlett-Packard XL cartridges are on sale now.

(5.) You save $12.00 per cartridge when you order this month and this is a great time to stock up.

(6.) Would you like to order those cartridges today?

Opening Statement Example
Real Estate Agent

1.& 2. Good morning, Mrs. Prospect, this is John Sellalot from GoodHomes Realty.

3. We specialize in finding buyers for homes within 30 days of the listing date.

4.& 5. The reason for my call today is last month your next-door neighbor's home sold at $10,000 above the appraised value.

6.   This would be a perfect time for you to get a complimentary personalized home evaluation report. Shall I prepare one for you?

Now that you have set the objectives for your call and written your attention-getting opening statement, it's time to start planning your powerful cold call!

Action Plan

Which part of this chapter will be most useful to you?

_____

_____

_____

_____

How will you use these ideas?

_____

_____

_____

_____

On what date will you begin using the ideas?

_____

CHAPTER THREE

Cold Calls

Special Skills

How many people do you know, who are successful at cold calling? It's a difficult thing: calling people who don't know you and whom you've never spoken with before. It takes a special skill to do this—and to convince this person to *buy* from you. So, a few months ago, when I heard from someone who bought because of a sales person's cold call, I decided to find out *why* she bought from this particular sales rep.

The Customer's Perspective

How do you get new business? Some companies use direct-mail marketing successfully. Others use a combination of fax blasts and direct mail marketing. But when effective telephone marketing is added, your sales can *skyrocket*.

Special skills are needed for really successful telephone marketing and not everyone is good at it. When I heard from someone (Ann Gaines) who bought toner cartridges from a specific business *only* after getting numerous cold calls from the sales person (Patricia Fisher), I asked Ann *why* she bought from this sales person—what set Patricia apart from other sales reps—and this is what she told me:

"Actually, it was her persistence. I kept putting her off. And she picked *one* item—printer cartridges. She simply asked me to get a price quote from her before I ordered from the discount store. And after I placed my first order, she sent me a fancy little thank you note in the mail!"

Secrets of Productive Cold Calls

I asked Patricia Fisher for her success secrets and this is what she said:

> "I think it is very important to believe in the product you are selling as well as the company you work for. When I am cold calling a customer I mention that I have been handling office equipment supplies for many years and I am very fortunate to be working at Bond Business Products.

Persistence Pays Off

"Be persistent! I tell customers that I don't expect to get all their business after one or two calls. Try us out. We will show you the type of service we provide; let us be an alternative to your current vendor—a back up.

"When I cold call and speak with the receptionist, and can't get through to the decision maker—I ask for the name of the person who is responsible for ordering office equipment supplies—I'm not trying to sell anything—I just want to send information. I then send an introductory letter to the decision-maker and information about our company.

"After I have a good cold call—I send a thank you note along with my business card. A lot of my customers say they like the 'note' they have received from us."

Six habits

that set Patricia apart as a sales professional

1. **She is persistent.** Even though the customer "put her off," she did not give up after only one or two calls.
2. **She picked one item to focus on.** She didn't confuse the prospect by talking about a variety of products.
3. **She believes in the products she sells** and the company she works for. That belief is communicated to her prospects.
4. **Patricia offers to be a _back-up supplier_** in case the customer's regular vendor doesn't have what the customer needs. This is a non-threatening soft-sell approach that I have seen pay off over and over and over again.
5. **She makes the first call just to get the name** of the decision- maker, then she sends an introductory letter with information about her company and products.
6. After a successful cold call, **she sends thank-you notes** with her business card. This is the mark of a professional. It sets Patricia apart from her competitors. A personal thank you note is remembered and appreciated by prospects and customers.

WORKSHEET # 1
Your Cold Call

1. Good morning [*prospect's name*] _____
This is [*your name*] _____

2. calling from [*your company*] _____

3. We specialize in providing [*type of business you are calling*] with [*benefits of your products/services*]

_____

_____

4. The reason I'm calling you today is that there is a possibility we

5. may be able to help you [*achieve benefits you offer with your product or services*]

(*Optional*) while at the same time [*eliminate or cut down on problems related to using the products/services.*]

---

6. How are your [*products/services*] _____ currently purchased?

Cold Call Example
Introductory Statement—Any Type of Business

(1.)   Good morning [*prospect's name*] I'm [*your name*] with

(2.)   [*your company*].

(3.)   We specialize in working with [*type of company you have worked with and are calling now*] in helping them to [*something they want to get or avoid*] so that they can [*results/benefits from using your products/services.*]

(4.)   The reason for my call is that

(5.)   We have a time-saving new [*type of program*] program for [*type of business you are calling*] and I'd like to ask a few questions to see if this might be of some value to you.

(6.)   How do you currently [*purchase or use the type of product/ service you sell*]?

WORKSHEET # 2
Your Cold Call

1. Good morning _____
I'm _____

2. with _____

3. We specialize in working with _____

in helping them to _____

so that they can _____

4. The reason for my call is that

5. We have a new _____

and I'd like to ask a few questions to see if this might be of some value to you.

6. How do you currently _____

Cold Call Example

Introductory Statement—Mortgage Broker

(1.) Good morning [*prospect's name*] I'm [*your name*] with

(2.) and (3.) [*your company*]. We specialize in providing low-interest mortgage loans for homeowners in your area.

(3.) and (4.) I'm calling you today to talk to you about some refinancing options that we have available for your mortgage loan.

(5.) We may be able to save you several thousand dollars, depending on your current interest rate. I'd like to ask a couple of questions to learn if this would be of value to you.

(6.) What interest rate are you paying now?

Always end your introductory statement with a needs-based question. This will cause the prospect to think, talk and become involved in a conversation with you.

Increase Sales with The Right Questions

Not long ago I received a call from my local cable company.

The caller proceeded to read from a script telling me about their new programs and services. Never once did he ask a question like: "What kind of shows do you like to watch?" or "Do you like to watch sporting events?" or "What kind of movies do you prefer—new releases or the classics?"

I listened to his script and when he was finished, he asked me if I wanted to order one of their services. I told him I wasn't interested and ended the call.

Selling What Customers Want or Need

It is so much *easier* to sell people what they want or need. How do you find out? Ask! If the cable man had asked me which movies I preferred to watch, he probably would have made a sale of several of the movie channel services. But since he never bothered to ask, he lost a sale.

Asking the Right Questions

According to marketing research, 86% of salespeople ask the wrong questions. As a result, they miss opportunities and end up wasting their time and customer time.

Results from the same research found that 95% of customers (16,000 customers were interviewed) say that salespeople talk too much.

When do you begin asking questions? You can start after you introduce yourself, your company and state the reason for your call.

Open-Ended Questions

You can say: "I'd like to ask a few questions to learn how our services can benefit you. How are your [*products*] currently being purchased?"

How can you find out which products or services your customers will buy from you? Just ask!

Cold Call Example
Introductory Statement—Selling Cable Service

(1.) and (2.) Good afternoon [*prospect's name*] I'm [*your name*] with [*your company*]. I'd like to thank you for being such a good customer.

(3.) and (4.) I'm calling you today to let you know about the newest cable services now available in your area.

(5.) We have several exciting new movie packages at a very low introductory price. I'd like to ask a couple of questions to find out which program you qualify for.

(6.) What kind of movies do you prefer—new releases or classics?

Getting Attention and Interest

The best telephone marketing call I ever received was from a well-known credit card company. Here is how it went after the caller identified herself and her company:

> *Caller:* "First of all I want to thank you for being such a good customer. We really appreciate your business."

> *(I liked that. I felt valued as a customer.)*

She continued:

> *Caller:* "The reason I'm calling today is that we are reaching out to our preferred customers to let them know about a special program we are offering."

> *(She had my complete attention. She didn't waste my time. She got right to the point. I was a "preferred customer" and it sounded as though I might benefit from this "special program." I was all ears.)*

The caller then went on to tell me about three of the benefits I would get if I upgraded to the *Gold Card*. These were money-saving benefits, including discounts with businesses I regularly dealt with. I upgraded.

> *This sales professional had my attention from the first sentence. She sounded professional. She immediately answered my mental "what's in it for me" question.*

One of the reasons this call was so effective was because of the caller's use of *positive power words*. Next, you will see 16 *positive power words* you can use to turn a stale presentation into a compelling dialogue between you and your prospect.

Positive Power Words

Research by direct marketers has found the following words get the best response from consumers:

▸ Entitle
▸ Quality
▸ Reward
▸ Save
▸ Preferred
▸ Exclusive
▸ Personalized
▸ Investment
▸ Program
▸ Support
▸ Flexible
▸ Powerful
▸ Alert
▸ Maximize
▸ Convenient
▸ Excellent

When you use at least one positive power word in your opening statement, you have a greater chance of getting the prospect interested and curious enough to want to remain on the telephone and continue the conversation.

WORKSHEET # 3
Your Opening Statement—
Using at least one *Positive Power Word*

_____

_____

_____

_____

_____

_____

_____

_____

Turn-Off Words

Just as there are *Positive Power* words that spark the interest of prospects, **there are also specific words and phrases that can cause a prospect to lose interest quickly.**

Think about the last time you received a telephone call from someone you didn't know. Specifically: a telemarketer. What was it about the beginning of the telephone call that caused you to realize it was a telemarketer calling to sell you something?

Here is an example of what turns off most consumers receiving an unexpected telephone call from a stranger:

Caller: "Hello. How are you today?"

If you are like most of us, when a stranger calls and asks "How are you?" you immediately feel that person is going to try and sell you something. Your guard is up. You may be thinking: "He doesn't even know me. He doesn't really care how I am." Right away you begin to think of ways to end the call. When calling someone you know, then it *is* appropriate to ask "How are you?"

Question: On a sales call, what works better than asking "How are you?"

Answer: Getting right to the point. Introducing yourself and your company and stating the reason for your call—including benefits for the listener.

Changing a Habit

Some may feel it is the polite thing to do—asking "how are you" at the beginning of a cold call. But consider how you feel when a stranger calls and asks "How are you."

Many sales people ask that question because it is a habit. But when those words are eliminated, you'll be surprised at how much better the response will be.

Sales-Killer Phrases

Some words and phrases used by sales people can change a customer who is about to buy into a non-customer who wants to end the conversation quickly. Certain phrases and words are almost guaranteed to kill a sale. For example:

✗ **"You *do* want to save money, don't you?"**
(Who wouldn't?)

✗ **"We can't do that."** (Instead, say: "In cases like this, what usually happens is . . .)"

✗ **"You'll have to . . ."** (Customer gets defensive with this one.) Better to say: "What I will ask you to do is . . ."

✗ **"You're confused"** or—"you're wrong." (Guaranteed to anger the customer.)

✗ **"That's not my department."** This is a phrase that sends the message: "I can't help you and we don't really care about your business."

When someone calls to inquire about, for example, a billing problem (and you don't handle billing problems) the better way to direct the customer to the proper person is:

> ☺ "The real expert in billing situations is [*insert name of the person who handles billing*] and I can connect you now or ask her to call you back. Which would you prefer?"

Beware of the deadly phrases and words that can kill the sale and lose the customer!

Are You Different from Your Competitors?

Do you have a competitor who sells the same products you sell? If that's the case, why should people buy from you and not your competitor?

Why *Different* is Important

Different is important if you have competitors selling the same products you sell at the same or a lower price.

Different is important because if customers can buy exactly the same products somewhere else, why should they buy from you?

It's not enough to BE different, you need to tell prospects **how** you are different and how they will **benefit** by buying from you.

KEY POINT: If you **don't** differentiate yourself (your product/ service) you may lose the business.

How to Differentiate Yourself

There are ways to communicate *how* your company is different without criticizing the competition. Examples:

- "Our customers tell us they like the fact that a *real person* answers the telephone at our office, unlike most businesses they call."
- "Our company has been recognized as one of this city's top 100 companies for nine consecutive years."
- "Our widgets are the only local ISO 9001:2000 Certified quality widgets that meet the International standard for quality assurance in design, development, production and installation."
- "We are the only local company that guarantees same-day delivery service."

Action Plan

Which part of this chapter will be most useful to you?

_____

_____

_____

_____

How will you use these ideas?

_____

_____

_____

_____

On what date will you begin using the ideas?

_____

CHAPTER FOUR

Responding to Objections

Do They Mean What They Say?

The late financier J.P. Morgan once said: **"People have two reasons for what they do—the reason they tell you and the real reason."** This is true with objections your prospects raise. You can't always take the objections at face value. For example, when they say:

> "We're happy with our current vendor," or
> "Your price is too high," or
> "Just send me a catalog,"

These objections may be smoke screens, hiding the real objection. They could really be thinking:

> "Why should I change?"
> "Will the quality be the same as what I'm getting now?"
> "Is this company reliable?"

Objections are often a value test. It's as if the prospect is saying to you: "Do you believe in what you're selling? Would *you* buy it?"

Get Past the Smokescreen

Before you make your next call, write down the objections you hear most often. Next to these objections, write down what the prospect may be thinking. Then, write down your response to what you feel the prospect may really be thinking.

You'll find that the answers you write for what they may be thinking will also work for the answers they give you. When you hear "I'm happy with my current vendor." Imagine they are saying "Why should I change?" and prepare your reasons why other prospects have switched over to your company and the benefits they have found after becoming one of your customers.

WORKSHEET # 4

Objections you hear most often

1._____
2._____
3._____

What the prospect may be thinking
(See Get Past the Smokescreen above.)

1._____
2._____
3._____

Your response

1._____
2._____
3._____

Objection: "Your price is too high."

"How can I sell my product if a prospect tells me that my price it too high?" This is what I hear at nearly every sales seminar. Would it surprise you to learn that **73% of consumers buy for reasons other than price?** Among the many reasons for a price objection there is another—unspoken—objection that may be difficult to handle, and it has little to do with price.

The price objection is so easy for buyers to use, that often, people use it just to end a conversation. **The price objection can mask the real objection**, which most people don't want to verbalize. No, this is not about *value* although perception of value is critical. This is about something else.

It's about a natural, human reaction to unpleasant past experiences. Whether it was the wrong decision when buying a stock, or a past experience with a car that was a "lemon," we have all made mistakes. **We learn from our mistakes, and we have a fear of making mistakes—a fear of taking a risk.**

One definition of risk: "Jeopardize." **Buyers don't want to jeopardize—or risk—their money or their reputation or their career.** So, as a seller, if you can remove the obstacle—the risk—from the buying experience before you hear an objection, you have a much better chance of earning the prospect's business.

Three Ways to Remove the Obstacle

1. **Begin building a relationship—building trust.** When the prospect trusts you, they are less likely to feel they are taking a risk by buying your products. They are more likely to become a customer.

   You can begin building a relationship by offering and sending free information—not sales or marketing information about your products, but free educational information.

   Another way to begin building a relationship—building trust—is to let your prospect know you are willing and available to answer questions about the products or services you are selling. This is especially important when selling complex or intangible products or services.

2. **Begin collecting testimonial letters from satisfied customers.** Nothing is more convincing to a prospective buyer than reading real, current letters from real people and real businesses who have used and are continuing to use your products or services.

   Testimonials are critical if you are selling products or services considered risky by consumers. Customers who have been burned in the past don't want to repeat an unpleasant experience.

   Providing current testimonial letters written on a customer's letterhead stationery will cause the reluctant prospect to think again, and realize that "hey, I guess if other people—other businesses—are using this product, (or service) it must be okay."

3. Another way to remove the risk—the obstacle to making a buying decision—is to **offer a 100% money-back guarantee.** Use the words "risk-free" in your guarantee.

Five Ways to Handle a Price Objection

It is exactly the same product, but somehow your competitor's retail price is just a fraction above the price you pay for the same product. There is no way you can lower the price without giving away all of your profit. What do you do?

1. **Tell the truth.** Admit that you can't be competitive on this particular product. The customer will respect you for being honest.

2. **Offer a generic or a compatible product if you have one.** It helps if you have a few testimonial letters from customers who are happy with the generic or compatible product you sell.

3. **Find out what ELSE they buy.** You can say for example:

"Unfortunately our price on the 51645A is not competitive, but we have a GREAT price on the 92298A. Do you need one of those today?"

4. **If they don't need anything today** tell them you will create a file listing the items they buy on a regular basis and ask if you can mail, fax or e-mail monthly sale information. This keeps the door open for future opportunities with this customer.

5. **Ask to be considered as a second or "back-up" source** for this and other products in the event their current supplier is out of stock.

Objection: "Your price is too high."

The C.I.A. Approach

There are three steps you can use to effectively handle a price objection. An easy way to remember these steps is to think of C.I.A. No, not the Central Intelligence Agency, but *C*ushion, *I*solate and *A*sk.

1. Before you say anything after you hear a price objection, use a *cushion* statement like "I see" or "I understand." Reason: This lets the prospect know you are not going to disagree or argue. (*Read more about cushion statements later in this chapter.*) Then immediately go to step 2.

2. *Isolate* the objection by asking questions to find out if there is another concern. If there is something else that is important to the prospect, like fast delivery, quality products, product knowledge or good service, you can focus on these benefits, rather than price.

To *isolate* the objection and find out what else is important to the prospect, you can ask:

1. "If it weren't for that, you would go ahead and order from us?" or

2. "Is that the main thing holding you back right now?" or

3. "Assuming we agreed on price, what else is important to you?"

Objection: "Your price is too high."
Response:

"I'm glad you mentioned price. That's one of the benefits of buying from [*your company*]. We will divide the total cost into installment payments, so your actual cost per month will be very low. You can take delivery next week and your payments won't start until next month. How does that sound to you?"

Objection: "It's too expensive."
Response:

Repeat the objection: "Too expensive?"
Then stay silent and wait to hear more of an explanation from the prospect. S/he will usually tell you what s/he is comparing your product and price to.

How to Handle Price Shoppers

Nearly everyone who is involved in sales has met a price shopper. Some prospects will price shop only once, until they get to know you, your company, products and service. Others will continue to grind you on price. How do you work with price shoppers?

Dangerous Discounting

To some consumers, price shopping is actually fun. It's something they do often and is almost considered a sport. But when it affects your business and your profit, it is not at all fun for you and can be dangerous for future business. Four points to think about when dealing with a price shopper:

(1.) If you are too quick to make price concessions, the

prospect's perception of the VALUE of your product may go down.

(2.) If you lower the price too quickly just to get the business, think about what effect this will have on your customer's attitude the next time s/he buys from you. Will s/he expect an even lower price?

(3.) Differentiate with value: Service after the sale, product quality, durability, delivery, stability of the company backing up the product, etc.

Closing Opportunity

(4.) If you drop the price, *immediately* ask for the order.

> *"If I can* get this price for you, will you place the order now?"

IMPORTANT: After you ask for the order, don't say a word until after the customer answers your question.

If the prospect answers "no" to this question, he probably won't buy from you at any price and it's best to let him go. Move on to the next prospect and don't waste any more time with this person.

Cushion Statements

What are cushion statements? They are non-threatening, "cushioning statements" used before directly answering objections. For instance: "I understand," or "I see." Example:

Objection:—"We buy our [*insert your products*] from your competitor, the XYZ Company."
Cushion statement: "I understand."

Response to Objection

"I understand. XYZ is a good competitor of ours" (you are validating their judgment.) "Some of my other customers used to buy [*insert your type of products*] from XYZ and what they found was, XYZ didn't stock [*insert specific products you stock*] We stock those products on a regular basis here in our warehouse in addition to most [*insert another type of products you stock*], so please keep us in mind as a second source. I can call you or fax you when your products are on sale. Okay?"

"And, by the way, do you need any [*insert products you sell*] today?"

"I understand" will work—as your first two words—when responding to most objections. It lets the prospect know you don't intend to argue.

Objection: "I'm busy now and can't talk."

Response: "I understand. When would be a better time to call you with new product information?"—Or—

Response: "I understand. If this is your busiest time of day, I can call you tomorrow afternoon. Or would Thursday afternoon be better for you?"

These responses are designed to get the prospect to think, talk, and become involved in a conversation with you. When that happens, you have a better chance not to get shut out at the beginning of your call, and to get your foot in the door.

Objection: "I'm happy with our current vendor." Response:

1. "I understand. Which [*products*] are you buying now?"—or:

2. "I see. Is it the quality you're getting there, or the service that you like best?"—or:

3. "I understand how you feel. Some of my customers felt the same way you do, and they found, after using our [*fill in your product or service*] they experienced much [better, easier, faster, etc.] [*fill in results*]."—or:

4 : "I understand. Customers who have switched over to our company tell us our [*fill in with your benefits, i.e., quality products, response time,* or service, *etc.*] is the best they've found."—or:

5. "I understand. Please keep us in mind as a second source. If your current supplier is ever back-ordered on an item you need, please give us a call. We keep those products in stock and can get them to you the same day you call us."—or:

6. "That's great! That gives you time to evaluate other resources, so you can have a second source for [*your products or services*] when your current vendor is not providing the results you need."

You are calling an inactive customer who hasn't ordered from you in over a year, and you hear:

Objection: "We don't need anything."
Response:

"I understand. When will you need to order again?" Or—

Response:

"I understand. Last year we had the opportunity to supply you with your [*insert products they bought from you*]. I'd like to ask a couple of questions to find out which one of our new programs you qualify for so you can decide whether it would be worth your while to take another look at what we could do for you. Okay?"

Objection: "We're all set."
Responses:

1. "Oh, so you're the person who does the buying for that?"
2. "I see. Which [products] do you buy?"
3. "I understand. When will you need to re-order?" or—
4. "I understand. When should I call you back again?"

Objection: "It's too complicated."
Responses:

1. "Yes, it is complicated and with our technical assistance you can learn how to use it in less than a week. We can deliver it to you on Tuesday—or would Wednesday be better for you?"
2. "My job is to make it easy for you. It will take only a few minutes to help you and your staff feel comfortable using it. Can I write up the order?"
3. "This is where you benefit from using our services. We are the only company in town that includes free training. And you can return for training in the future as often as you like, at no charge. We can enroll you in the class beginning on Monday. Would you like to do that?"

Objection: We buy everything from one source.
Response:

"I can understand how you feel, some of our other customers felt the same way you do. They found that the one source they ordered from didn't **specialize** in any one product. Our customers like the fact that our focus is on [*insert type of products you specialize in*] and service. Because we specialize in [*insert type of products or service you specialize in*] customers feel more comfortable ordering from us, knowing that if there is ever a problem with their [*insert machine or hardware*] we can fix it. We are responsible for their [*insert machine or hardware your company services.*] They didn't have that assurance from the other company they were ordering [*insert your type of products*] from. May I send you our monthly sale flyer?"

Objection: "We tried this product before and it didn't work well for us." Responses:

1. **"I understand how you feel.** I have customers who felt the same way, but after using our [*products with description of benefits*] they found [*more benefits*]. Improved technology and manufacturing methods allow us to offer you a very high quality product. I can send you a [*product*] to evaluate—okay?"

2. **"What happened?"** (Find out exactly what happened when they tried a similar product in the past. Then describe how your product is different.)

3. **"I'm sorry you had a bad experience.** I've had similar experiences with products that didn't work. I can assure you that our product is completely different than the one you tried. And it is 100% guaranteed. Here is how our product is different: (explain how your product is different from what they tried in the past.) I can send you one to evaluate, okay?"

Objection: "The XYZ widgets are better." Response:

1. "I understand. Some of my best customers used to own the XYZ widget. I can fax the names and telephone numbers of my customers who are now using our widget. What is your fax number?"

2. "Obviously, you've had a chance to look at the XYZ widget. What did you like about it?"

CAUTION: This second response can be risky unless you follow up on their answer with this statement:

"On a scale of one to ten, with ten the highest, how would you rate the XYZ widget?"
If their answer is anything but a 10, ask this question:
"What would it take to make them a 10?"
Their answer to this question will tell you what you need to do to earn their business.

Objection: "Your Shipping Costs are Too High." Response:

"We would love to lower the freight charge, but we're simply passing along our shipping cost and that allows us to give you the low price you're getting. What we can do is double the order and with the quantity discount, you would save $16. How does that sound to you?"

Objection: "Just send me a catalog." Response:

"Let's look together right now, at our web site catalog."
This accomplishes three objectives:

1.) It **keeps the phone conversation alive and active—** keeps the dialogue going.
2.) Gets the prospect **physically involved in the conversation.**
3.) Helping the prospect scroll through your company's web site is a good way to easily **present and introduce additional products** the customer may not have been aware of.

Objection: "Just send me a catalog."
Response:

"We used to send catalogs and found that as soon as they were mailed, many of the prices had changed. What we do now, in a situation like yours, is find out which items you are interested in and fax current information just on the products you use. Okay?"

Objection: "Business is slow now.
We aren't buying anything."

Layoffs and Downsizing

It can be discouraging—making call after call and hearing sad stories about why people are not buying now. The words *Layoffs* and *downsizing* have become all-too-familiar words in our vocabulary. If you sell luxury products, this may be an especially difficult time for you. But if you sell items that are necessities, there are ways to motivate consumers to *want* to listen to what you have to say about your products.

If you stock less-expensive generic or compatible items, you have an advantage in a slow economy. You can offer a cost-saving product for people who need to cut back on spending.

You cannot disagree with any statement regarding the sluggish economy. Anybody not living in a cave has read newspapers and watched television with dramatic news stories about corporations in serious trouble. Every day we hear about businesses downsizing and laying off hundreds—even thousands of employees.

So, what do you say to someone who tells you their company is laying off employees and this is not a good time to talk about buying anything? Or if you hear: "Because of the economy, we aren't buying now. Call us back in a few months."

Response:

"Yes, the economy is slow right now and because of that, I wanted to see if your company qualifies for our new cost-saving

Buyer's Choice Program with an extra bonus for qualifying by February 5th." [*You can call your program whatever you feel is most appropriate for your products/service.*]

Then ask a needs-based question like "How are your [*products*] purchased now?" (Who wouldn't want to qualify for a new cost-saving program?)

Or: "Because of the current economic situation, we're offering a new Starter-Pack to introduce our premium [*products*]. How many [*products*] do you use each month?" Be sure to end your statement with a needs-based question so you can get the prospect involved and talking.

A New Way to Look at Objections

There are many different ways to handle objections. Each sales professional has her/his own technique. Last year I heard an unexpected response to an objection which resulted in a sale. This sales person's response to the objection may surprise you.

Obstacles Can Become Opportunities

One day last year I made the rounds of several neighborhood shops to pick up a few necessities before leaving for a trip out of town. One store I visited was *Radio Shack*—to buy audio tapes for an upcoming sales seminar. As I stood at the cash register and handed my money to the sales person, she asked me: "Do you need a cell phone today?" I answered: "No. I have a cell phone."

That was a pretty definite objection, right? That statement would have stopped most people. It did *not* stop this sales professional. She immediately said (in a cheerful voice): "We offer both Verizon and Sprint service." Then she showed me her "favorite cell phone."

She (her name was Janice) had no way of knowing that for nearly a year I had been unhappy with my current cell phone service and that I had been thinking of switching to Sprint, but had put it off until I had time to make the change.

Janice broke most traditional selling rules. She did not acknowledge my objection. She did not use a cushion statement, like "I understand," before responding to my objection. What she *did* do, was turn a $16 sale into a $180 sale—by telling me what Radio Shack could provide in the way of cell phone service.

Before I walked into that store, I had no thought of switching to a new cell phone service on that day, or purchasing a new cell phone. But on the theory that every consumer is a prospect, this sales person persevered and ending up selling me something I really did want, but had not made the effort or taken the time to buy.

Can You Read Minds?

How can you know if your prospects might want or need your products/services? How can you know if your prospects may not be happy with their current provider? Answer: You cannot possibly know until you:

▶ Ask,
▶ Suggest, or
▶ Let them know what YOU have to offer.

Try it For a Week

Find out how this method of handling objections can work for you. Every day this week—when someone voices an objection—give her/him a fact/benefit relating to your products/services. It may just result in a sale for you!

One Little Word Makes a Difference

Research indicates that you can double the amount of

information you get from a prospect if you begin your questions with one specific word.

People will only buy when they feel comfortable with you, your company and your products or services. When they feel uncomfortable, they **won't** buy.

If you are uncertain about why a client has said or done something, don't phrase your clarifying questions using "Why." Instead, use the less challenging "How."

Examples

Questions like:

✗ "Why did you change the schedule?" or
✗ "Why did you decide to buy from the XYZ company?"

Sound like a demand. Prospects may feel defensive with questions phrased this way. Instead, use the following:

✔ "*How* did you decide to change the schedule?" and
✔ "*How* did you decide to buy from the XYZ company?"

The "how" questions ask the prospect to describe actions, not justify their decisions. Because the phrasing is perceived as less threatening, it has a much better of getting the information you need. The difference between *how* and *why* is the difference between conversation and interrogation.

The Three-Letter Word Never to Use

There is one word, used in everyday conversation, which can derail an otherwise perfect sales presentation. This one little word is often used when responding to an objection, and it can ruin everything else you say.

Use *and* instead of *but*

If a customer has a concern, listen and acknowledge that concern. Using the word **but** negates everything you've said before it. What your customer hears is the disagreement that precedes an argument.

Instead, first acknowledge the concern and follow with the word "and." Example:

> *Customer*: "This process sounds complicated."
>
> *Sales Rep*: "Yes, it is complicated and (instead of *but*) with our technical assistance, you and your staff will be experts in less than a week. We can deliver one to you on Thursday; how does that sound to you?"

Action Plan

Which part of this chapter will be most useful to you?

_____

_____

_____

How will you use these ideas?

_____

_____

_____

On what date will you begin using the ideas?

_____

CHAPTER FIVE

Winning the Sale

How to Turn First-Time Callers into Buyers

Did you ever get a phone call from someone who was just looking for information about your products or services? Someone who found your web site or advertisement and called to "just get prices" from you and then they didn't order?

Recently I called to get information about a specific service I needed. It was the first call on my list of four similar businesses that I intended to call (shopping around). But I ended up buying from the FIRST company I called.

After looking through the Yellow Pages for a chimney sweep company, I carefully made a list of four businesses whose advertisements looked good. When I called the first, *Magic Chimney Sweep*, a friendly (human) voice answered the call. One point in their favor—I didn't get a recording right away.

After I said I was calling for information and pricing, she asked for my address. I could hear the sounds of keystrokes on a computer keyboard as she entered my home address. After a few seconds she said: "Oh, this is good—you qualify for a discount because in 1985 we cleaned the chimney for Cathy Daniel at your address !"

I was very impressed with their record-keeping; I purchased my home in 1986 from Cathy Daniel.

A Good Reason to Buy

She went on to say: "The regular price is $95.00 for a chimney cleaning, but because we performed this service once before at your address, your price is only $79.95. We can send someone this week—which day would be best for you?"

WOW—In less than 30 seconds she gave me a good reason to buy—a discount. But—and this is important: It was not a discount available for just anybody. **It was a specific discount based on past purchasing history.** That made it credible and believable.

And I had the reassuring feeling that this company was stable. After all, they kept customer records for at least 15 years. AND she asked for the order!

Why I Didn't Shop Around

1.) The sales person had a positive attitude and a friendly voice,

2.) I was very impressed with the fact that they kept accurate records for 15 years. That made an immediate connection and was a real attention getter.

3.) The accurate record-keeping gave me the feeling that I was dealing with a reputable company. I had the perception that this was not a "here today, gone tomorrow" business, but a stable, reliable company.

4.) I was given a benefit and a good reason to buy during the first few minutes of our conversation—a discount based on past history.

Golden Opportunity

When a prospect calls you for information, that person is much more receptive to buying from you than he would be if *you* initiated the call. They are calling you at their convenience and have made three very important decisions:

1.) Which product/service they need,

2.) The decision to spend money, and

3.) The decision to call YOU

Create a Buying Opportunity

How can you make a connection and create a special buying opportunity for the prospect that calls you for the first time—if they have no purchasing history with your company?

After finding out which product or service they are calling about—if you have price flexibility—you can create an immediate discount based on either:

- ✔ Any product they want. You can offer a "First Time Caller" discount, or
- ✔ If they are calling about a specific product—and if there is enough profit margin in the product, you can call it a "Today's Special [*name of product*] Discount," or
- ✔ If there is not enough profit margin in the product they are asking about, and there is enough profit in a "companion" product, you can create a "Purchase with Purchase" discount.

They Want to Buy

When people call you, they want or need to buy something you sell, otherwise they would not have called. So the easier you can make it for them to buy from *you* (without giving away too much profit) the better your chance to make a sale and begin a new customer relationship.

Ten Ways to Ask For The Order

Marketing studies have found that—except for customers calling specifically to place an order—only 3% of prospects actually offer to buy, telling you: "That sounds good; I'll take it" or: "Okay, you've got yourself a deal." The remaining 97% wait for you to ask them to buy.

Closing Questions

Different ways to ask for the order include: The *choice* close, the *you'll save* close, the *direct* close and the *trial* close.

Choice Close

- "Do you want delivery to your warehouse or your office on Main Street?"
- "Do you want the standard service contract or would you like more comprehensive coverage?"

"You'll Save" Close

- "You used 6 of these last month, and you'll save $10.00 by ordering a dozen. Shall I send 12 out to you today?"

Direct Close

- "I can get it there tomorrow. How many would you like?"
- "Can I write up the order?"
- "How many do you need today?"
- "I know you're going to be happy with this chair. Can I turn in your order today?"
- "We have a truck going into your area on Friday and I would love to put your cartridges on it. Shall I write up the order?"

Trial Close

- "How does that sound to you so far?"
- "Am I going in the right direction?"

One reason a trial close works well is because a trial closing question asks for an opinion and not a decision. Opinions are easier to give than decisions. After a trial close question, a prospect will often say: "That sounds good. Send me a dozen." But if you only hear: "That sounds good," you'll need to follow up with a direct close question.

Three Reasons to Use a Trial Close

1. You are getting feedback from the customer without actually asking for the order.
2. You are taking pressure out of the sales situation because **you are not asking the customer to make a decision.** You are only asking your customer for his/her opinion.
3. **An opinion is easier to give than a decision.**

Low-Risk Strategy

At first it may feel uncomfortable to ask the prospect how s/he feels about your product or service. But remember: **you run little risk with trial closing.**

The trial close can be used any time during the selling process to test the waters. **The purpose of the trial close strategy is to help you know when to ask for the sale.** Sometimes the answers you get are so strong that you won't have to close at all—you'll just naturally write the order.

One of the most successful sales people I've worked with used a trial close more often than any other type of close. In fact, I began listening more closely to her sales calls because I noticed that she rarely asked for the order, yet **she was consistently at the top of the sales chart each month.**

Call Script Examples

Find out time frame

Sales Rep: "When you are making a decision of this kind, what is the procedure you typically go through and how long does it take?"

Qualify Prospect's Decision—Making Process

"How many people would ultimately be involved in making a decision to proceed?"—or

"Who else besides you would be involved in the decision-making process?"

Ending the call

"Just one other question. In case I can't get in touch with you during normal business hours, are you ever reachable earlier in the morning or later in the afternoon at your direct extension?"

(RESPONSE YES) **Sales Rep:** "And that number is?"

(RESPONSE NO) **Sales Rep:** "What is the best time of day to contact you?"

Sales Rep: "I have your address down as [*prospect's address*] Is that correct?"

(Response)

Sales Rep: "Good! Thank you for your time and have a great day."

Call Script Example

*Following up on lead for interest in
home-based health product business*

Sales Rep: "Good morning *Mrs. Jones*. This is *Mary Smith*. I represent *Home Health Program* and I have your name from our web site sign-up form.

"*Home Health Program* is a research and development company that markets a line of natural health products offering a terrific opportunity for someone interested in a profitable home-based business. Are you still interested in a home-based business?"

(Response no.)

Prospect: No, I'm not.

Sales Rep: "I see. Would you like me to send you a brochure on our products in case you decide at a later date you would be interested?"

Prospect: "No."

Sales Rep: "Thank you for your time today."

(Response yes.)

Prospect: "Yes. I'm still interested, but I'm not sure how this would work."

Sales Rep: [*Explains benefits of product/business*] "and you can get started for as little as $10.00. How does that sound to you?"

(Response no.)

Prospect: "I'm not ready to make that commitment now."

Sales Rep: "I understand. I'll mail a brochure to you with this information so you will have it when you decide you want to think about this again. Okay?"

(Response yes.)

Prospect: "Okay. I guess that sounds pretty good."
Sales Rep: "Great! Which credit card would you like to use today?"

Cold Call Script

Sales Rep: "May I speak with Mr/Ms [*prospect's name*] please?
Prospect: "This is he (she)."
Sales Rep: "Mr/Ms [*prospect's name*], this is [*your name*] with [*your company*]; (Verify decisionmaker) Do you take care of (or "do the purchasing of") [*products you are selling*]?
Prospect: "Yes."
Sales Rep:

    "Good! [prospect's name], we specialize in saving time for [*appropriate department*] and freeing up additional resources to be used on [*other company responsibilities*]. Our [*your product/service*] enables companies to [*solutions your product/service provides*]. Would this be something of interest to you?"

(Interested) **Prospect:** "Well, I would need to take a look at it— could you fax or mail me some information about your company and the product?"

(Response to get an appointment)

Sales Rep: "Yes I can. However, I will be in your area next week and could show you an actual demonstration of how our [product] can work in your office. That would give you a better idea of how the [product or service] would benefit your department. It would only take about 10 minutes. How does that sound to you?"

(Response to schedule the next phone call)

Sales Rep:	"Yes, I would be happy to send you some information. If I send this out today, you should get it within five business days. You will need about an hour to review it and write down some questions. When will you have time to do this?"
Prospect:	"Probably by next Friday afternoon."
Sales Rep:	"Great! I'll call you the following Monday, the 8th. Would morning be best for you or is the afternoon a better time?"
Prospect:	"Monday afternoon around 3:30 would be best."
Sales Rep:	"Good. I'll call you on Monday at 3:30."

(No Interest at all) **Prospect:** I'm really not interested.
Sales Rep: Thank you for your time today.

Two Little Words

In a controlled experiment by a restaurant, servers were asked to use two specific words throughout customers' meals.

Cocktails, the menu, wine lists, fresh ground pepper, the dessert tray, were all offered by the server, who used the words *for you.* "Shall I order a cocktail for you?"

The results were significant. The servers involved in the experiment reported that **their tips increased by 20% after they started using the words *for you.***

Considering the power these two little words hold, you may want to incorporate these words into your presentations. Here are some ideas:

"Here's the proposal I developed for you."
"I have a special offer for you."
"I think we'll be able to make an exception to that policy
for you."

"These are the shipping options we have prepared for you."

Two Words Calm Irate Customers

A successful customer service representative in Dallas, Texas uses two words when a customer calls with a problem or a complaint. The two words are: "Thank you."

"Thank you for calling to let us know about this."

Why should you *thank* a customer for complaining?

Because if s/he didn't come to you with the problem, s/he might take it to one of your competitors.

This customer service rep expresses her empathy with serious problems by saying "That's terrible!" Then she assures the customer that she's going to do whatever it takes to solve the problem.

WORKSHEET # 5

Call Planning Sheet

Your objectives for this call _____

_____

1. Greeting and identification—your name, company name.

_____

2. Ask to speak to a specific person by name

_____

3. When the correct person is on the telephone, repeat step one and then make a connection (current or former customer) or use an attention-getting opening statement explaining what your company does.

_____

_____

4. Reason for the call _____

_____

5. Benefit statement _____
_____

6. Question relating to a need _____
_____

7. Listen to answer.
8. Acknowledge answer, respond to objection and follow up
with questions _____
_____

9. Sales message with benefits _____
_____

10. Close _____
_____

EVALUATION FORM

What action will you take as a result of this call?
_____
_____
_____

What action will your prospect take?
_____
_____

What did you learn during this call that will affect the way you
handle the next call?
_____
_____
_____

On what date will you follow up with your prospect? _____
Additional comments about this call
_____
_____

When Is It Time to Stop Selling?

Last month I received an e-mail from someone who asked:
"How will I know when a prospect is ready to buy? Are there any
specific words to listen for?"

That is a very good question, because it's important to know when to stop selling and when to start asking for the order.

A recent 15-year study found that 80% of salespeople failed to close the sale when the buyer was ready to order!

There are sales reps who have literally bought their product back from a prospect because they kept talking and selling after the prospect was ready to buy. If sales people do not recognize buying signals, they can actually talk their way out of a sale.

When a prospect says something or asks a question that sounds as though they are interested, it is time to stop selling and ask for the order. You may hear questions like:

- "How soon could I get it?" or
- "When can it be delivered?" or
- "Is it available in another color?" or
- "Which credit cards do you take?"

All of these questions could be buying signals. **If a prospect is not at all interested in buying from you, they would not ask these questions.**

Buying Signals

If you are not sure that what you have heard is really a buying signal, ask a "testing question." The conversation could go something like this:

Prospect:: "How soon could I get it?"

Sales Rep: "Most of our products are shipped next day. How soon do you need it?"

Prospect: "How many would we need to order to get the quantity discount?"

Sales Rep: "You will save $10 each when you order two. Or you can save $15 each when you order four. Which would you prefer?"

Ask for The Sale

If the prospect says: "We have been thinking about trying a new supplier in the future" or "I guess that sounds like a good idea," then it is time to ask for the order, saying something like: "We can ship it out today and you should get it tomorrow. Okay?"

When you recognize buying signals and respond appropriately, you will save yourself selling time and make more sales faster.

The Secret to Closing More Sales

What characteristics do most successful salespeople share? Researchers for the *Behavioral Sciences Research Press* studied sales production for more than 25 years. Their work revealed that most successful salespeople share two characteristics:

(1.) They contact more prospective buyers than less successful salespeople do.

(2.) They ask for the order more often than less successful salespeople do.

Habits of a Sales Star

Linda Benson is one of the most committed and talented sales people I have ever known. She increased sales of office equipment supplies—to end users—from zero to $60,000 a month in 18 months. Linda attributes part of her success to a motivational sign she placed on the top of her computer monitor that reads: *Ask for the sale*. After you read the statistics below, you will probably want to put the same sign on your computer.

Consider these research findings:

● 46% of salespeople ask for the order only once before giving up.

- 24% ask twice before they shy away.
- 14% give it a third try.
- 12% are brave enough to ask a fourth time before they quit.

The interesting thing about this research?

The same study revealed that more than 60% of all sales occur after the salesperson asks for the order FIVE times—or more.

What that means to you: You may hesitate to ask for the order. You don't want to come across as a high-pressure sales person, but keep in mind that **asking for the order is what you need to do to succeed in sales.**

Action Plan

Which part of this chapter will be most useful to you?

_____

_____

_____

How will you use these ideas?

_____

_____

_____

On what date will you begin using the ideas?

_____

CHAPTER SIX

Thank You Letters

Thank-you Letters

How often do you get a handwritten thank-you note or letter? If you have ever shopped at a Nordstrom store, you have probably received such a letter. Part of Nordstrom's legendary customer service includes the regular use of handwritten thank-you notes to customers. Very impressive.

Follow-up Letters and Calls

If you want to come across as a professional and be remembered after your initial sales call to a prospect, send a follow-up letter. The purpose of the letter:

✔ Thank the prospect for her time on the telephone
✔ Enclose information, price lists, catalog, etc.
✔ Remind the prospect of the date and time you will be calling back to discuss the information you sent.
✔ Remind the prospect of additional benefits of your product or service.

Thank-you Follow-Up Letter
After cold call

Date

Name, Title
Company Name
Address

Dear [*Customer's Name*]:

Thank you for your time today. It was interesting to learn more about your company and the success you've had over the past ten years.

Enclosed is the additional information you requested on our products and services.

As we discussed on [*Day you spoke*], I will call you on [*Day and date*] at [*Time*]. to discuss your company's situation and how our [*products or services*] can help you [*benefits and solutions your company can provide*]. I look forward to talking with you next week.

Sincerely,

[*Your name*]
[*Your title*]

Enclosure: Product information

Thank-You Letter

Date

Name, Title
Company Name
Address

Dear [*Customer's Name*]:

Thank you for the opportunity to work together on your [*service you provided*]. It's been a pleasure assisting you with this time-saving and cost-saving service.

Enclosed is information about new products and services now available, which you may want to add in the future. I appreciate your business and will give you a call in a few weeks to check in.

Sincerely,

[*your name*]

Enclosure: New products and services brochure

Thank you letter

Date

Name, Title
Company Name
Address

Dear [*Customer's Name*]:

Thank you for giving me the opportunity to provide you with [*products or services you provide*]. I sincerely appreciate your business. I hope that your experience with [*name of your company*] was a pleasant and rewarding one. If I can be of service to you again in the future or if you ever have any questions, please feel free to give me a call.

As a [*your products/services*] Specialist, I strive to serve each client in a professional manner, with a high degree of competence and proficiency. I hope that my service met or exceeded your expectations.

[*name of your company*] offers the full array of [*products/services*] to serve the needs of [*geographical area or type of business*]. The success of our business, as with any business, largely depends on referrals from previous clients. I would appreciate you recommending my name to others you know who may have a need for [*your products/services*].

I will be happy to answer any questions you have in the future.

Sincerely,

[*Your name*]
[*Your title*]

P.S. I thank you in advance for your future business and referral recommendations

<<>>

Customer Appreciation Letter
to current customer

Date

Name
Title
Company
Address

Dear [*name of prospect*]:

We want to take this opportunity to thank you for your business. We appreciate your business and the opportunity to serve you throughout the year. A true, solid commitment to outstanding customer service is the thread that runs through every aspect of every department here at [*your company name*]. Our goal is to always meet your needs in the best way possible.

As part of our thanks, we invite you to use the enclosed savings coupon chosen just for you. I hope you will take us up on this special promotion and the savings you will realize.

Just call us today at [*your telephone number*] to take advantage of this money-saving offer with absolutely no risk.

Thanks for the opportunity to serve you again and for your continued confidence in [*your company name*].

Sincerely,

[*your name*]
[*your title*]

Enclosure: Savings Coupon

<<>>

Thank-You Letters
For Referral

(Handwritten is preferable.)

Date

Dear [*name*],

Just a quick note to thank you for the referral to [*prospect's name*]. As a result of your referral, I [*state a result or the current status, for example: scheduled an appointment, met with them*]. I will keep you posted on the outcome.

Thank you again for thinking of me and please let me know how I can be helpful to you.

Sincerely,

[*your name*]

Dear [*customer's name*]:

Thank you for your kind offer to give me business referrals. As we discussed, I am enclosing three of my business cards. I thank you in advance for giving them to three of your friends or business associates. You can be sure that anyone you refer to me will receive the highest degree of professional service possible.

Sincerely,

[*your name*]
[*Title*]

Action Plan

Which part of this chapter will be most useful to you?

_____

_____

_____

How will you use these ideas?

_____

_____

_____

On what date will you begin using the ideas?

_____

CHAPTER SEVEN

Follow-up Calls and Letters

The Importance of Follow-up Calls

When making follow-up calls, always remind the prospect of your last conversation. Example: After sending information to a prospect, one way to begin a follow-up call is with enthusiasm. "After we spoke last Wednesday, I sent you the information we talked about and I've been looking forward to getting some feedback from you." Then, don't say a word until the prospect speaks.

Use action words to move the conversation forward.

Action words

- ▶ Recommend
- ▶ Suggest
- ▶ Discuss
- ▶ Plan
- ▶ Review
- ▶ Introduce

When you use action words, you will sound like a professional.

Example:

"Based on our last conversation, Mr. Jones, I recommend that you order _____ for your _____ because _____."

What not to say during a follow-up call:

✗ "Did you get the brochure I sent?"
✗ "Did you read the information?
✗ "I'm just calling to make sure you got my catalog."

When you ask questions like these, you risk getting a "no" answer and the conversation may quickly end. Instead of asking these questions, talk about what you would have talked about if they had read the information you sent.

Script for the Follow-up Call

Follow-up calls are critical because that's when most sales are won or lost. The second call should

(1.)   Remind the prospect of the first telephone call and
(2.)   Outline the objective of the return call.

The second call opening is as important as the first one. One way you can begin your call back is with the phrase "I'm calling to . . ." Complete the sentence with an action word to move the conversation along. Open with "I'm calling to" recommend, suggest, discuss, introduce, plan or review. Another way to begin the call: "As you remember from our conversation last Tuesday . . ."

Example:

Salesperson: "Hello Nancy, this is Kevin Chapman calling from Ace Paper Company. As you remember from our last conversation, you and John were going to review the information I sent you and today you and I were going to discuss plans to inventory your supply of copier paper to determine which size paper you need to order next."

WORKSHEET # 6
Your Follow-up Call

Write below an example of a sentence you can use in your follow-up call, using one or more action words.

_____

_____

_____

_____

_____

_____

_____

_____

_____

10 Words That Bring New Customers

There are two forms of marketing that will consistently add new customers to your database—without cold calling. One is direct-mail marketing, which is used by millions of businesses. The second form of marketing is often overlooked, yet it can provide you with a steady flow of new customers without cold calling and it's *free*. A sales professional in New Jersey finds new customers every week by using this second form of marketing on a regular basis.

Do You Hate Cold Calling?

If you dread picking up the telephone to call new prospects, you are not alone. Studies show that 40% of sales veterans experience call reluctance serious enough to threaten their continuation in sales.

If you are among the 40% of people with call reluctance, you can replace cold calling with another form of marketing. This will take only a few extra minutes each day. All it requires is motivation and a decision on your part to say ten extra words to at least one customer every day.

Free Marketing

Nancy Davis, a sales professional in New Jersey, told me this:

> "We always ask for referrals from our existing clients and we get them on a regular basis. It's really not as hard as you think. Watch for opportunities. When someone says: 'You guys give such quick service,' I'll answer 'thank you, and who else do you know that could use our products?'

Nancy goes on to say: "I have customers who regularly call me now and give me names. All I know is that *asking* for the business *works*."

Create a Habit

To find new customers starting today, say these 10 words to at least one customer:

"Who else do you know that could use our products?"

When you stop to think about it, **everybody** knows somebody else who could use your products or services.

This can become a habit if you choose to make it one. If you start asking for referrals today, you can begin adding new customers today.

The Disappearing Prospect

Have you ever sent a proposal to a prospect and then never heard from him again? Or sent a free sample of your product to a prospect to evaluate and afterwards you were unable to reach her on the telephone?

It Sounds Promising

You make the call and have what you feel is a productive conversation about your products or service. Or they call you, appearing to be interested in your products or service. They ask for a proposal and you have all the information you feel you need, so you take the time to develop and mail a proposal. Or you agree to send a free product for them to use and evaluate. And then . . .

The Vanishing Act

You don't hear from them. You call to follow up and they are "in a meeting," or "not available to take your call." You leave a message. You don't get a return call. You call and leave another message. And another. After awhile it becomes obvious. Your prospect has either been kidnapped, died, or somehow vanished from the face of the earth, leaving no trace behind. Or, most likely, they are procrastinating. They have put off reading your proposal or trying your product. Or their plans have changed. Whatever the reason, you need to find out what the situation is, so you can either cross them off your list or continue to follow up.

Preventive Maintenance

What can you do the next time, to make sure your prospect doesn't disappear? Here are some tips:

- Get the names of additional contacts within the company. During the first conversation, ask: "Who else is involved in the decision-making process?" Or: "Who else in your company should I talk to about this?" If they answer: "Only me," ask for the name of their assistant or secretary in order to "complete the file for your company." Get AT LEAST one other name—preferably two or three additional names of people you can contact in the future (in the event your prospect does a disappearing act.)

Getting Commitment

● Get a commitment before you send anything, whether it's a proposal or a brochure or a product to evaluate. Examples:

1. "I'll make a note to follow up with you next week.

   Or will two weeks be better for you?" Whatever they answer, *reconfirm* the date. If they say three weeks is better, you can say: "Good. Let's make plans to talk in three weeks and I'll call you on March 11th. What is a good time for you?" After they answer, say: "Great. I'll call you at 9:30 on March 11th. Okay?" End the call by repeating the date and time of your telephone appointment.

   "I have you on my calendar for a 9:30 a.m. telephone call on March 11th and unless I hear from you otherwise, I will call you then."

   Include the date and time for your telephone appointment in the note you send with your proposal or brochure or sample of your product.

2. "After you review the proposal, what is the next step in the process?" Then use example # 1 above.

OR—

3. "After you try our product and if it works well for you, when will you be placing your order with us?" Then use example #1 above.

Key Point

Don't just agree to send something without a commitment for a follow-up action. Make a definite appointment to follow up on a *specific date* and *time.*

Follow-Up Letter
After cold call

Date

Name, Title
Company Name
Address

Dear [*Customer's Name*]:

Thank you for your time on the telephone today. Enclosed is the brochure you requested about our [*insert your products or services*]. There are three important points about the services we offer:

1. [*Most important benefit your company provides*].
2. [*100% risk-free guarantee, etc.*]
3. [*Local company, 24-hour response time, etc.*]

Benefits like these are the reason we have so many satisfied customers since [*insert year*]. Here's what a few recent customers had to say about their experience:

> [*Testimonial from happy customers with name and company name*]
>
> [*Testimonial from happy customers with name and company name*]

I look forward to meeting with you on Thursday afternoon, March 27th at 3:00 p.m.

Sincerely,

[Your Name]
[Your Title]

<<>>

Follow-Up Letter
After cold call

Date

Name, Title
Company Name
Address

Dear [*Customer's Name*]:

You've taken the first step to [*benefit your products or services provide*]. Enclosed is the information you requested on our [*insert your products or services*]. I'd like to highlight three important points you'll find in the enclosed information:

1. [*Most important benefit your company provides*].
2. [*100% risk-free guarantee, etc.*]
3. [*Local company, 24-hour response time, etc.*]

Benefits like these are the reason we have so many satisfied customers since [*insert year*]. Here's what a few recent customers had to say about their experience:

> [*Testimonial from happy customers with name and company name*]
> [*Testimonial from happy customers with name and company name*]

I hope once you've had a chance to look over the enclosed information, we can count you among our happy customers.

Please don't hesitate to give us a call at [*Your telephone number*]. We will be happy to answer any of your questions or concerns.

Sincerely,

[*your name*]
[*your title*]

Enclosure

Follow-up Letter
After Customer's Inquiry

Date

Name
Title
Company
Address

Dear [*name*]:

A while back you took the opportunity to inquire about [*your product/service*]. I'm writing today to let you know that since we were last in touch, we have added [*your new products/services*]. I would love to have the opportunity to show you the many ways we can help you [*how your products/services can help the prospect*].

To celebrate our new product [*your company name*] is offering a free [*free gift to customer with low cost to your company*] should you decide to order [*your product/service*] by [*ending date no more than 30 days from today's date*].

[*Name of prospect*], take just a few minutes and call us today. We would be happy to provide all the additional information you need. Please call me at [*your telephone number*] to set up a convenient time to have one of our representatives stop by.

Thank you again for your interest in [*your company name*].

Sincerely,

[*Your name*]
[*Your title*]

P.S. Be sure to call before [*ending date of free offer*] to get your FREE [*bonus gift*]

<<>>

Letter Requesting a Testimonial

Dear [insert customer's name]

You recently ordered [insert your product/service] and I hope you're finding [it or them] useful and effective for your business.

Now, I'd like to ask a favor of you.

I am in the process of putting together a list of testimonials—a collection of comments about our [insert your products/services] from valued customers like yourself.

Would you take a few minutes to give me your opinion? There's no need to compose a letter. Just jot your comments on the attached form, sign and fax it back to me at [insert your fax number].

And if you'll be kind enough to give me your comments, I'll be pleased to return the favor by sending you a free [gift with high retail value but low wholesale cost].

I look forward to reading your comments about our [insert your product/service] and I welcome any suggestions.

Sincerely,

[your name]
[your title]

Fax Back Testimonial Form

Fax to: [*insert your fax number*] anytime, 24 hours
Please write your comments and sign below:

_____

_____

_____

_____

_____

_____

_____

_____

_____

[*Insert Your Company's Name*] has my permission to quote
from my comments and use my name and business name in
testimonials.

Signature: _____

Print Name: _____

Company Name: _____

Date: _____

Action Plan

Which part of this chapter will be most useful to you?

_____

_____

_____

_____

How will you use these ideas?

_____

_____

_____

_____

On what date will you begin using the ideas?

_____

CHAPTER EIGHT

Voice Mail Messages

In the past few years, voice mail has become very important for telephone sales people. Recent studies have found that up to 40% of outbound telephone marketing calls end up in voice mail. The words used in a voice mail message are just as important as the words used in the opening statement of a telephone call. Your message can be an effective sales tool or it can cause you to lose opportunities. Here is an example of a short—and to the point—first call:

> **"Good morning** *[insert customer's name]*. **This is** *[insert your name]* **calling from** *[insert your company]* **about an exciting new program** *[insert program/plan/benefit or sale offered by your company]* **through** *[insert ending date]*. **At your convenience, please call me at** *[insert your telephone number]*." (Repeat your name and telephone number.)

This is an attention-getting message because the caller:

☎ Talks about something new,
☎ Uses a positive power word *(program)*,
☎ Uses an ending date, as an incentive to call back.

Voice Mail to Persuade Prospect to Take Next Call

"Hi! This is [your name] calling. I just spoke with your assistant, [name of assistant]. I'm sending you some material on how you can benefit from using [your product or service.]

"It will arrive by E-mail today. I will give (assistant's name or prospect's name) a call on Friday. We can really save your organization time and money. If you are interested, please reply to my E-mail with a convenient time to call you. Or if you prefer, you can call me at [your telephone number]. Thank you for your time."

General Informative voice mail

"Good morning/afternoon. This is [your name] with [your company]. We specialize in (short sentence—less than 35 words—with benefits/solutions your company provides). I have some information available on [special offer or monthly sale] and will be sending it to you by mail to the attention of [contact name if known]."

"I will be following up on [insert specific day]. If you have any questions, my name again is [repeat your name]. You can reach me at [your telephone number]. Thank you very much for your time. I hope to speak with you soon. That phone number again is [your telephone number.]"

Attention-Getting Voice Mail from Mortgage Company

Hi [prospect's name]. This is [your name] calling from [name of mortgage company].

"I'm calling you tonight to talk to you about some refinancing options that we have available for your mortgage loan. My records show that we can save you several thousand dollars by lowering your interest rate and if you would like to learn more, please call us at [*your telephone number*]. That's [*your telephone number*]. I will call you back in a few days."

The Voice Mail Roadblock

Marketing and selling by phone can be the most successful and cost-effective way to connect with customers. But voice mail is one **roadblock** that can discourage even the most optimistic telephone professional. It can really be frustrating: Day after day, making call after call after call only to end up in voice mail. And often you don't get a call back after leaving your message.

So, how can you stay positive and get your message across, despite the voice mail roadblock?

If you have left two or three messages and you don't get a call back from the customer, remember not to let your exasperation and frustration show in your voice.

Following is an example of a third or fourth voice-mail message you can leave for the customer who did NOT return your call:

The call back *after you've spoken once* to the prospect or customer but have not received a call back and you have called and left additional voice mail messages.

"**Good morning** [*insert customer's name*]. **This is** [*insert your name*] **from** [*insert your company*]. **I'm calling to follow up on our** telephone conversation on [*insert date*] about [*insert product/ service you spoke about*]. **I'm sorry we've been unable to connect but I want to let you know that** [*insert time-sensitive benefit., i.e., "sale ends on the 30th of this month,"*] **and I would hate to see you miss out on this opportunity. At your convenience, please call me at** [insert your telephone number]." Repeat your name and telephone number.

If the account is very small or you feel the potential is not there, don't waste your time and energy leaving multiple voice mail messages.

The Almost Perfect Voice Mail Message

One day while I was out of the office, I received a call from someone (her name is Judy) who works for the company that publishes a magazine I subscribe to. Her voice mail message sounded good; she was clear and articulate. But something was missing. I don't know her and have never spoken with her before, but she had a very nice, friendly voice.

Judy used the right words—almost. The reason for her call: My subscription to her magazine is about to expire. She was calling to ask if I wanted to renew. But **she did what nearly 50% of telephone marketing people do: She did not use her last name.**

Why use your last name? Using your last name sends a clear message of professionalism. Not using your last name diminishes the importance of your message. This was Judy's message (with company name changed):

"Hi Ann, my name is Judy. I work for the Smith Publishing Group. You've been subscribing to our magazine for the past three years. Your last issue is due to ship in August and I'm checking to see if I may send the renewal invoice to you. It's ninety-nine dollars for the year. My telephone number is (she stated her telephone number clearly). Can you give me a call today with your decision? Thank you, Ann."

Some telesales people may think that using only a first name on a voice mail message sounds friendly. But **if the prospect does not know the caller, not using a last name can cause confusion and waste time for the prospect. Using first and last name builds credibility and adds to the perception of professionalism.**

More on Names

In the space of one week, I received one excellent voice mail message, two that were a waste of the callers' time and one that was almost unbelievable.

The two that were a waste of time might have been okay except that both callers raced through their calls, and then left *only* their first names, which were unintelligible. One name sounded like "Garmarah," and the other caller's name was pronounced quickly and sounded like "Flipper." Because I was planning to write an article about voice mail, I decided to return both calls. I found out that the first caller was named Tamara and not "Garmarah." I learned that the name of the second caller was not "Flipper," but Skipper, an unusual name for a woman.

An Effective Message

The best voice mail that week came from someone who spoke very clearly and left an attention-getting voice mail message. The message she left is below. (I've replaced real names and telephone numbers in the message with fictitious names and not a real telephone number.) The message went like this:

"Hello Ms. Barr, my name is Mary Jones and I'm with Congressman John Smith's office in Washington. We're recruiting business leaders like yourself, to help us with the President's stimulus package. We would like to talk to you. Please call me today. Again, my name is Mary Jones and I can be reached at 1-800-555-0000. That's 1-800-555-0000. Thank you."

This call was effective because:

▸ **It was short, direct and to the point.**
▸ **She sounded professional, positive and polite.**
▸ **Her words were very clear and easily understandable and she repeated her name and telephone number twice.**

An Almost Unbelievable Voice Mail Message

The last voice mail message was left by someone who sounded very self-confident and his message sounded interesting. Up until the time when he yawned. Yes, he actually YAWNED in the middle of his voice mail message. (Did he think that couldn't be heard??) If the caller was so bored by his own message, you can be sure I was **not** interested in calling him back.

How Does Your Message Sound?

If you're not sure how your own voice mail message sounds, a good way to find out is to call your office or home and leave yourself exactly the same message you intend to leave for your prospects.

WORKSHEET # 7

Your Voice Mail Script

1. **Greeting and identification—prospect's name, your first and last name, company name.**
"Good morning (or afternoon) [prospect's name] _____
"This is [your first AND last name] _____
"calling from [your company] _____

2. **Reason for the call and benefit statement**
"I'm calling to _____
_____

3. **Ask for a call back**
"At your convenience, please call me at [your telephone number] _____
4. **Repeat your name and telephone number**
"Again, this is [your first AND last name] _____
"And my telephone number is [your telephone number] _____
"Thank you for your time."

Action Plan

Which part of this chapter will be most useful to you?

_____

_____

_____

_____

How will you use these ideas?

_____

_____

_____

_____

On what date will you begin using the ideas?

_____

CHAPTER NINE

Beware of Telephone Burnout

Avoiding Telephone Burnout

Even though increasing the number of sales calls is a key to success, too many calls can leave you with *telephone burnout*. Telephone burnout can result in:

▶ Finding every possible excuse not to make phone calls
▶ Inventing tasks that will keep you too busy to make outbound calls
▶ Leaving the office to call on customers you really don't need to call on, wasting valuable time.

(I know this because I have been guilty of all of the above.)
How do you learn how many phone calls can result in telephone burnout? By on-the-job experience and by trial and error. Each person is different. I've known sales reps who can make 50 to 75 phone calls a day, five days a week—and not burn out. On the other hand, unless your time is managed very well, too many phone calls will mean you won't be able to keep up with administrative responsibilities like updating files and checking on back orders. And not everyone can sound as cheerful, positive and energetic on the 75th phone call as on the first call.

Reduce Fatigue

Here is something I did which helped to avoid burnout: I made half of my phone calls standing up. Physically, the voice sounds a little different when you stand up. Your voice will feel stronger and making calls standing up will make you feel more energetic and you will sound more enthusiastic.

Standing up occasonally will reduce the fatigue that comes from sitting too long by boosting blood circulation to your back and legs.

Motivation Matters

Last year I spoke with a sales person who was new (one week) on the job and was feeling discouraged. She said when she makes sales calls, she feels as though she is "bothering" customers. Now, I know for a fact that the people she calls *use* the type of products she sells and *need* the products she sells. I told her that there is a way to change the way she feels, before she makes sales calls.

Rejection Can Be Painful

I experienced the same feelings when I started out in sales. After a few "I'm busy now" answers, and "We don't need anything" responses, I found myself making fewer and fewer calls. Someone once said, "It's not rejection that hurts, it's how you react to rejection that hurts you."

An Inspiration

Fortunately, the person in the office next to mine was an inspiration and a role model. I listened to her making calls and at first I thought she was calling her friends or family. She sounded equally as happy to be talking to the person on the other end of the telephone—no matter who it was.

It was the same with incoming calls. The same cheerful attitude and friendly tone of voice. And she sounded sincere. As I got to know her, I realized she *was* sincere. She truly liked people and loved her job.

As I listened to Kathy on the telephone, I learned that no two calls were exactly the same. That gave me an idea. I decided that if I made each call different from the next, I would look forward to making the calls and my voice would sound more enthusiastic when I enjoyed making the calls. And then I found new ways to motivate myself. What I learned can work for anyone.

Six Tips to Motivate Yourself

1. To motivate yourself, **make the first call** in the morning **to a customer already buying from your company**—someone you like and you know is a happy customer. Tell yourself that everyone you call that day will be just as happy to hear from you.

2. **Plan ahead of time exactly who you will call and why.**

3. **Write down your main objective for each call**, so you will know exactly what you want to accomplish with each call.

4. **Write down second and third objectives** in case the first objective doesn't work out. This way, no call will be a total loss, unless the person you call is not available.

5. **Set a goal for each day**—the dollar amount you want to sell for the day. Using a black magic marker, write that number BIG on an 11 by 17 piece of paper and tape it up on the wall where you can see it clearly.

6. If you do experience rejection and/or objections you are not able to overcome—say this out loud after the call is over:
"NEXT." Meaning: It's time to move on to the next call. Clear the slate and make the next call on your list. Tell yourself that the person you just called was *not* rejecting y*ou* personally or your products. Tell yourself they are

having a bad day and probably are not feeling well. Then, make the next call.

It is amazing what can happen after you *tell* yourself that you *like* the people you call and that they will be happy to hear from you. After all, your company is reliable and your products and services are the best, right?

After you plan ahead, write down your objectives and put your sales goal up on the wall, you'll find your attitude will improve, your voice will sound better and customers will be more receptive. And remember what the successful entrepreneur, Mary Kay Ash, said: "If you think you can, you can. If you think you can't, you are probably right."

Are You Too Successful?

The price of success can be high. When a sales person does everything right, including making numerous outbound sales calls every day, giving customers the best possible service and building long-term relationships, incoming calls—not related to sales—may increase.

Non-Sales Calls

When you get non-sales related calls from your customers, this is evidence that you have been very successful at building good business relationships and customer loyalty. They feel free to call you with a variety of questions, requests and problems.

Unfortunately, one by-product of your hard work and success may be that you now have very little time to make outbound sales calls. Customers will begin to call you with all sorts of requests and problems, including:

▶ Service and support issues

▶ Billing problems

▶ Questions and problems not directly related to sales.

Billing and Service Quetions

When a customer calls to ask a billing-related question normally managed by your accounting department, a good way to handle the call is to say: "When it comes to billing situations, the real expert is Katie Jones in accounting. Can you hold on while I connect you?"

If you do not normally handle service or support requests, these questions can be handled the same way.

Follow Up

Since the call came first to you, you are responsible for following up with the customer. Call the customer back to find out if their concerns/questions have been answered, *after* verifying with the appropriate department that the customer was helped and the problem solved.

Make sure you are not guilty of one of the seven deadly sins in customer service—telling a customer who calls with a problem: "That's not my department." This answer tells customers you are only interested in talking with her/him when they want to buy something and that you are not concerned about them, otherwise.

It's a real opportunity when customers call with a question, problem or complaint. Unhappy customers who don't complain, often stop buying from you. Consumer research by the A.C. Nielsen Company found that *only two percent* of unhappy customers complain, while a surprising 34 percent of dissatisfied customers simply find another supplier, without letting the current vendor know about problems.

Finding Time

If you find yourself overwhelmed with non-sales related

incoming calls, it's time to re-evaluate your objectives and look carefully at how you spend your time during the day. In other words: look at your other time-robbers—not just externally imposed time robbers, but those which are self-generated. You may find that you can carve additional hours out of your day to make outbound sales calls by eliminating or cutting down on self-generated time robbers that can lead to telephone burnout.

Action Plan

Which part of this chapter will be most useful to you?

_____

_____

_____

_____

How will you use these ideas?

_____

_____

_____

_____

On what date will you begin using the ideas?

_____

CHAPTER TEN

E-Mail Marketing

Instant Results Marketing

A few years ago, if someone had told you that you would soon be able to use a low-cost marketing technique that would yield an immediate 5%, 10% and even a 30% response rate, you probably would not have believed it. But it's true.

What is this amazing marketing tool? It is opt-in (permission) e-mail marketing.

Who uses opt-in e-mail marketing? To name just a few high-profile companies: The New York Times, Amazon.com, Microsoft, The Wall Street Journal, Omaha Steaks, Motorola, and the list goes on and on.

Obstacles to Success

How could something that can be amazingly successful, (if it's used the right way) also make enemies—when it is used the wrong way? Here's how . . .

There are basically two types of e-mail marketing:

(1.)   Unsolicited e-mail, and
(2.)   Opt-in (permission) direct e-mail

Unsolicited e-mail can get you into a lot of trouble. What kind of trouble?

✗ When you send marketing e-mails to prospects or customers *without* getting their permission first, you risk losing that customer forever. Consumers and business professionals are bombarded by unwanted, unsolicited e-mail. According to research by 1-to-1 Magazine, the average U.S. online user will receive 738 unsolicited e-mails this year and more than double that by 2006. When marketers use e-mail addresses of those who have not given permission, they run the risk of consumer backlash.

✗ Many Internet service providers will discontinue your account when they get complaints from angry recipients of your unsolicited e-mail.

How to Begin

E-mail is used to attract customers the same way that postal direct mail is used in the offline world, with one big difference: Permission must be received from the customer. The online world does not tolerate unsolicited messages.

Ask for Permission

If you haven't already, begin asking your customers for their e-mail address and permission to send them e-mails with:

▸ New product information,
▸ Advance notice of monthly sales,
▸ Change in pricing and/or
▸ Monthly e-mail newsletter.

Use Your Website

Put a sign-up form on your web site and offer an incentive for visitors to send you their e-mail addresses. Motivate readers to opt-in by offering something special when they sign up. **On my web site, www.SellingSupplies.com, I offer a free report** *64 Ways to Increase Your Sales,* **when visitors subscribe to my "Weekly Sales Tips"** e-mail newsletter. My database of e-mail names and addresses grows larger every week.

Newsletter Benefits

Carl Cobb, vice-president of sales at Asay Publishing, publisher of RS&R News at www.rsrnews.com said: "We see a 20% increase in the hits on our web site on the afternoon of—or morning after—the day we send out our weekly e-mail newsletter."

Customers Become Involved

There are two different types of e-mails you can send to your customers:

- A once-or twice-a-month informational newsletter with helpful hints and tips and no sales or marketing content, and
- A once-a-month marketing e-mail, separate from the newsletter.

When both types of e-mails are used—and the informational e-mail contains valuable and useful information—your marketing e-mails are more likely to be welcome and read.

Nothing can take the place of a personal letter or e-mail. The written word makes a human and emotional connection. When customers read your e-mail messages, they become instantly involved. They start thinking about you and your company, products and services.

Amazing Benefits

When e-mail marketing is used the right way, the benefits are astonishing.

1.) **Fast.** As opposed to direct-mail marketing, you can send thousands of e-mails in minutes.

2.) **Instant results.** Minutes after sending your marketing e-mails, you can start seeing responses and getting orders.

3.) **High Response Rates.** If your e-mail message is well written and sent to the right people at the right time, it is not unusual to see 5%, 10% and even 30% response rates.

4.) **Low Cost.** No printing or supplies cost, no postage, no time spent folding, stuffing, sealing and stamping direct—mail letters.

Customer Retention

Recent marketing research has found that 27% of customers switched vendors because their sales representatives lost touch. Your competitors are contacting your customers, so it makes sense to use every means available to stay in touch with your customers.

Don't Get Deleted

As opposed to your informational monthly newsletter, the successful e-mail sales message must contain 12 components. Unless you integrate all 12 of these ingredients, your message may get . . .

- ✔ Immediately deleted or
- ✔ Forwarded to your ISP as spam or
- ✔ Filed away for future (non) action.

Plain Text or HTML?

Do your customers prefer HTML or plain text e-mail messages? Look at these statistics from a recent survey by *Opt-in News*:

- 62% of consumers prefer plain text e-mail messages
- 35% prefer HTML (Hypertext Markup Language)
- 3% prefer Rich Media (Macromedia Flash and Shockwave, with various audio and video formats.)

This is good news for marketers because plain text is easier and less costly to create.

12 Critical Ingredients

Unless you include all 12 of the following components in your e-mail marketing message, your e-mail may get immediately deleted.

1. **Get their attention.** Use a compelling subject line, like:

   - "How to avoid becoming a victim of fraudulent telemarketers"
   - "Three tips to sell your home faster."
   - "Do you recognize the seven early warning signs of a copier breakdown?"

2. **Identify the problem.** Help them to feel the pain of a problem you can help to prevent or fix.
3. **Provide solutions.** Tell the reader how you can solve the problem.
4. **Show the benefits.** Sell the sizzle and explain the benefits to the customer.
5. **Include testimonials.** A very convincing and extremely powerful selling tool. Use real contact names and recognizable company names.
6. **Make an irresistible offer.** Use an attractive combination of price, terms or free gift with purchase. Raise the value by adding on products or services instead of lowering the price.
7. **Guarantee your product or service.** Give the strongest

guarantee you are able to give, like: "100% risk-free guarantee."

8. **Time limit or scarcity.** People are more motivated to act by the fear of loss than gain.

9. **Call to action.** Use action words like: "Call us today at [your telephone number]" or "click on the link below to order now" (or "to get more information.")

10. **Personalize.** Just as a direct mail letter addressed to "Occupant," or "Office Manager," has a 50% chance of being thrown away, an e-mail message not personalized with the contact name may be viewed as spam and deleted.

11. **Add a P.S.**—Repeat the offer with time limit or scarcity. Research has found there is a startling increase in response when a P.S. is used.

12. **Use an opt-out sentence.** At the end of your e-mails, always use an opt-out sentence like: "If you do not wish to receive further e-mails . . ." or "if you would like your name removed from our list, please reply to this message with 'remove' in the subject line."

Important: After receiving a "remove" request, be sure to delete that name and e-mail address from your database.

Adding Value

An e-mail newsletter will add value because you have knowledge and expertise about your products and services that your customers do not have. In a short, one-page e-mail newsletter you can provide helpful hints and tips. **Example:** You can use an attention-getting headline, like: "Your printer has enemies" and explain how to take care of a printer to keep it running smoothly.

Cost Effective

The list of companies utilizing opt-in e-mail marketing is huge and growing every day. Why? Because—dollar for dollar, it is the most cost-effective way a business can produce revenues literally overnight.

Be Careful What You Write

Not long ago I received an e-mail from the CEO of a Fortune 100 corporation. With all the resources in the world at his disposal—including the money to pay for the best copywriters, it is surprising that this CEO didn't enlist the aid of an expert to write his e-mail marketing message. (You won't see the name of the CEO here, or the name of the company that sent the E-mail.)

Following is the first paragraph:

> "I spend a lot of my time thinking about how [*name of his corporation*] can do a better job of serving its customers. I'm convinced that we need to do more to establish and maintain broad connections with the millions of people who use our products and services around the world. We need to more thoroughly understand their needs, how they use technology, what they like about it and what they don't. I'd like to share with you some of what we've recently begun to do."

This well-known CEO forgot two of the first rules of direct marketing and business communication.

The First Rules

(1.) **Leave yourself out of the message.**
Count the number of "I's" (the *first* word in the message is "I" and the 6th word is "my.") In the first paragraph, the word "you" appears only once. The words "I," "my," "we," "I'm," "our," and "we've" appear *nine* times.

(2.) **Write as though you are writing to only ONE person.**
One person at a time will be reading each message received. Instead of "their needs" and how "they use"

the service, the words should have been "your needs" and how "you use" the service.

If readers were able to get past all the "I's," "we's" and "our's," the rest of the message didn't get any better.

Example of a Good E-Mail Message

The writer of the following e-mail used a friendlier and more personal style of writing—directed to just *one* person:

> "Dear Ann: Last month you requested information about a new fax machine. Great news: This week you can take 10% off the price of any one of the fax machines at [*web site address*]. This special offer is good through February 28th and you won't find a better value anywhere. Please call me at [*writer's phone number*] and we will reserve one of these top-quality fax machines for you."

This message contains four "you's" and only one "me." *Much* more effective than the CEO's message.

A Personalized E-Mail

This next E-mail sounds like it came straight from the heart.

> "Dear Ann: This special was just announced and I wanted to let you know about it ASAP. These prices are great and prices have never been this low. To take advantage of this special before it ends on Friday, call me today and your order will be processed while the special is still on. When you call, ask for Marie and I'll make sure we take great care of you."

With the words she used, the writer managed to convey the impression that she cared about her clients. Marie did three more things very critical in marketing:

(1.) She let the reader know that the special "ends on Friday," and

(2.) She *asked for the order,* and

(3.) Even though Marie sent this message to hundreds of people, **it looked as though it was written to only *one* person.**

Action Plan

Which part of this chapter will be most useful to you?

_____

_____

_____

_____

How will you use these ideas?

_____

_____

_____

_____

On what date will you begin using the ideas?

_____

CHAPTER ELEVEN

Keeping the Customer

It's very painful when you lose a customer. And if you don't know why the customer left, it's especially troubling. But if you have lost a few here and there, you are not alone.

If you keep all of the same customers year after year after year, you are in the minority. Consumers are being bombarded with telephone calls, faxes and e-mails from your competitors. How do you keep customers?

Regular telephone contact is crucial if you are selling renewable services or consumable products. But staying in touch with your customers does not always need to be only by telephone. Direct mail, e-mail and fax is another way to maintain contact with customers. Here are five tips:

1. Send monthly sales flyers by mail or fax and write a short note in the margin. **Example: "I thought of you when this sale was announced," or "I hope you can take advantage of this sale—this is a great price!" Writing a note on the flyer makes it seem more personal, not like they are one in 1000 people who received the flyer.**

2. Send a flyer with information about a product the customer is not currently buying **from you. They may have put you in a niche and feel you only sell one type of product.**

They may not be aware of all the products and services you offer, that they *could* be buying from you.

3. Send new product announcements whenever you add something new. **Write a personal note on the announcement.**

4. If fraudulent telemarketing is a problem in your area, call or send a personalized letter **or e-mail to your customers advising them of the problem and how they can avoid becoming a victim.**

5. **Send a personalized letter to customers** when there is a change in personnel in your company. Customers will appreciate that you took the time to let them know and it makes them feel they are part of your office family.

Retaining Customers

In a recent marketing study, entrepreneurs were asked what their greatest concerns were, in having a successful business. The number one answer? 66% said that retaining customers was their biggest concern. **And yet many businesses spend more time going after new accounts than they spend contacting and re-contacting current and past customers.**

The results of another marketing survey: 27% of customers switch vendors because their sales representatives lost touch.

Getting Sales That Belong to You

If your customers are buying—from one of your competitors—some of the products *you* sell, that means someone else is getting sales that belong to you. Make sure your customers are aware of *all* of your company's capabilities. Your satisfied and loyal customers may be willing to buy additional products or services from you—if they *know* about everything you can provide.

How to Make the Big Bucks

Here is a great quote from Michael LeBoeuf, Professor of Management at the University of New Orleans:

> "The big bucks aren't in making customers. They are in *keeping* customers."

Building Customer Loyalty

Finding new customers is challenging. *Keeping* customers is *critical*. A sales rep in Texas has a special way of communicating to customers that their business is valued.

Making a Difference

In Amarillo, Texas, Leslie is described by her friends as having a "sunny disposition and a positive attitude." She is the same with customers on the telephone, making nearly non-stop sales and prospecting calls, averaging 60 to 75 completed calls each day. But it's not just the number of calls that's most important. It's what she says during the calls that make a big difference in her sales.

What She Says

Leslie sells office equipment supplies and calls each of her customers once a month, every other month or every third month, depending on their usage of the products. Her customers feel *special* and *valued* because Leslie makes every conversation unique. When she calls to let a customer know their products are on sale, instead of saying: "I'm calling to let you know your Canon fax cartridges are on sale," she makes it more personal. After reviewing their ordering history, she calls and tells the customer:

"I thought of you yesterday when this special price was announced, because you use two a month. While these products are on sale, would you like to order six? You'll save $36.00 and you won't need to worry about running out."

The phrase "I thought of you" sounds as though the call was carefully planned and is one of a kind, not one of a hundred. We all like to be *thought of*.

Worrying Pays Off

When Leslie calls customers and explains that she will be calling on a regular basis to check on their supply needs, she tells customers: "*I worry about your supplies, so you don't have to.*"

It's understandable that Leslie is at the top of the sales chart every month.

How to Notify Customers About a Price Increase

Good communication between you and your customers is essential to maintaining customer loyalty. One situation where the way you communicate becomes crucial is when you notify a customer about an increase in price. The way this is handled can either strengthen or damage customer relationships.

4 Steps to Handle a Price Increase

Last week I received this e-mail: "I have a customer that I'm selling a specific product to with a very low price. How can I increase the price without an objection? By the way, the price for this product has been increased by the manufacturer." My answer to this question: The best way to handle a price increase—

1. Give at least one month's notice.

Reason: The customer will appreciate the advance notification and will be more tolerant of the price increase if s/he has received prior notice. Suddenly increasing prices without any advance notice could destroy any trust you have built. Some customers may be annoyed to the point that they will take their business elsewhere.

2. Don't use a memo or letter. Instead: *call* and tell the customer about the price increase.

Reason: A memo or a letter notifying a customer of an increase in price is impersonal and may leave the impression that the customer's business is not important enough for you to make a phone call. The personal touch of a telephone call leaves a better impression.

3. Give customers a good a reason when explaining the increase (example: your price from the manufacturer was increased.)

Reason: Customers will be more understanding if you give them a reasonable explanation for the price increase.

4. Give the customer options, like a quantity discount, or an annual agreement, where they would agree to buy a certain quantity of the product during the next year for a specific discount.

The Hidden Obstacle

You make call after call, prospecting for new customers. You send out sales letters and marketing flyers to attract new prospects and keep in touch with current customers. But there may be a problem within your own company—you are not aware of—that could be driving away the business you have worked so hard to get.

Survey Finds Angry Customers

Telephone marketing and direct mail marketing takes time and costs money, but it pays off. You can connect with new prospects and keep in touch with current customers by using smart marketing. Unfortunately, while you are looking for new business and staying in touch with current accounts, some of your customers may be unhappy with one important element of your company.

According to a survey by Prudential, some of your customers may be irritated or even angered by your telephone system. They could be suffering from "Phone Rage." Results from this survey found that some phone systems annoy customers more than they help them.

If you are not sure how your company's telephone system is perceived by your customers, you may want check and make sure your system is not causing the problems found in the Prudential survey.

- 71% of people interviewed for this survey said that most of the time they must listen to **too many recordings** before they can talk to someone.
- 41% said they are too often **transferred to too many others** after they do reach someone.
- **40% reported becoming angrier by the minute** when trapped in voice mail or left on hold.
- 33% criticized recorded messages as **confusing or not right for their situation.**

Are Your Customers Annoyed?

To make sure your telephone system is not irritating your customers, call your company from a telephone outside your office and listen to how the call is answered. Ask yourself the following questions:

1. Is the call answered in less than three rings?
2. Does a real, live person answer the call?
3. If the call is answered by a recording, is there an escape route during the first sentence, like "dial zero to reach an operator"?

Phone Rage

If you can answer *yes* to at least two of these questions, your customers are probably happy with your current system. A good way to find out how your customers feel about your telephone system is to **ask** them. Most people will be more than happy to let you know how they feel. And **you will keep more customers** by making sure your telephone system is not contributing to *phone rage.*

How to Outclass the Competition

According to an American Management Association study, only 65% of customers buy every year where they bought before. Two recent buying experiences illustrate one of the reasons why 35% of consumers do *not* buy every year where they bought before.

Words Your Mother Taught You

Two simple words seem to have been forgotten by inexperienced clerks and sales people. Two words that nearly every mother teaches her child when the child first learns how to talk. These same two words—when used by a clerk or sales person—can make a big difference in the way consumers feel about a buying experience. From the time we were small children, our mothers taught us always to say "thank you."

Great Customer Service

Solid business relationships are nurtured with superior customer service. Nordstom is one company that is famous for outclassing its competition and keeping a loyal customer base. Their customer service is legendary.

Recently I went to three different departments in a Nordstrom store. In all three departments, I received the same respectful and courteous treatment.

- The sales person said "thank you" when I handed her my credit card.
- The same sales person said "thank you" after she had wrapped and handed the purchases to me. And she didn't just put the package on the counter; she walked around the counter and presented them to me while smiling and saying "thank you."

I look forward to shopping again at a Nordstrom store.

The underlying Nordstrom culture and philosophy is simple: Give great customer service.

A Different Buying Experience

Later in the same day, after I spent nearly $300 at another store, the clerk put the package on the counter and said: "You're all set. Have a nice day." Not "thank you."

I won't rush back to that store again.

Creating a Positive and Lasting Impression

By remembering to say thank you to customers, we build credibility, establish rapport and create a positive and lasting impression.

And, in addition to making our customers feel appreciated, there is another reason why we should say thank you; it helps us. When we express gratitude, we experience a brief moment of contentment. In a world full of uncertainty and trouble, we pause to enjoy what we have.

Action Plan

Which part of this chapter will be most useful to you?

_____

_____

_____

_____

How will you use these ideas?

_____

_____

_____

_____

On what date will you begin using the ideas?

_____

CHAPTER TWELVE

How to Win Back the Lost Customer

Sometimes, despite your best efforts to provide top-quality products and world-class service, you may lose a customer for one reason or another. What do you do? What do you say to find out why the customer left and—how can you earn the business again? Here are some ideas:

Script When Calling the Lost Customer

Sales Rep: "I've studied your account (or reviewed your file) and found that it's been [*length of time since they last purchased*] since your company last purchased your [*products they bought from you*]. I'm concerned that you may be running low on [*insert products*]. Shall I send you a case today?"

Or:

Sales Rep: "Last year we had the opportunity to supply you with your [*products they purchased from you*]. I'd like to ask you a couple of questions and give you new information about benefits we now offer, so you can decide whether it would be worthwhile for you to take another look at what we could do for you in the way

of [*type of products they bought from* your *company*].
Okay?"

If that doesn't work, the following question should get an
answer from the customer:

Sales Rep: "I know that not every company is perfect in every
way. If there were a way you feel we could improve
our products or our service, I hope you will tell me
what that is. I would really like to know because I
value our relationship (or: I hate losing your
business.)"

After you say this, don't say a word until the customer speaks.
If all else fails, send the customer the following letter.

Bringing Back The Lost Customer Letter
to Inactive Customer No Longer Buying from You

Date

Name
Title
Company
Address

Dear [*name*]:

It bothers me to lose a good customer; that's what compelled
me to write.

Not long ago, you decided to discontinue purchasing [*products
or services*] from [*your company name*]. I'd personally like to ask
you to reconsider your decision.

First, let me share what we hear from customers like you who
switched to another company—and have now switched back to

[*your company name*]. Many tell us they were simply not getting the same good service they got with [*your company name*], nor did they get the savings they expected.

Here's another real difference. With the [*your company name*] [*special program you offer*], you enjoy the convenience of [*benefits of your program*], which means you'll never again [*experience inconvenience*] [*of not having benefits of your program*]. You'll benefit from a substantial savings on [*savings experienced by using/buying your program/services/products*].

Finally, the enclosed savings coupon is yours to use as you please. Simply call us at [*your telephone number*] by [*ending date of special offer*], and order any [*products or services*] you need. We look forward to serving you again and earning your business.

Sincerely,

[*your name*]
[*your title*]

Enclosure: Savings Coupon
Valid through [*date—no more than 30 days from date of letter*]

Letter to Re-Activate the Lost Customer

Dear [*customer's name*]:

We Have a $15.00 Reward For Your Next Order!

Thank you for ordering your [*products*] last [*date they last ordered*]. But because you haven't bought any [*products*] since then, we are confused and perplexed. That's why we've decided to write you with this offer.

If there was something wrong with your last order, or if you weren't pleased with our service, please tell me because I want to know so we can fix it.

However, if that wasn't the case and you've been meaning to

give us a call for your [*products or services you provide*] and it's just slipped your mind, then I want to extend an invitation to you.

Please accept our $15.00 credit good towards your next order. No strings attached, no minimum order requirements and no obligation to buy from us again.

Why are we doing this? Simply put, we want your business again and we know from experience that once most companies start to buy once or twice from our company, they'll continue buying over and over again. Here's all you need to do to use your credit with us:

1. Call [*your telephone number*] to place a risk-free order for anything in our product line.
2. Your invoice will arrive with $15.00 automatically subtracted from the total.
3. Then if you're not completely satisfied for any reason, simply return the product within 30 days for a full 100% no-questions asked refund or replacement.

We know you have lots of choices when purchasing [*products/service*] and that's why we're sending you this $15.00 coupon for the opportunity to put us to the test. One important point: This savings voucher expires [*date—not more than 30 days away*]. So don't miss your chance to save $15.00 on your next order.

I look forward to welcoming you back as a regular customer again.

Sincerely,

[*your name & title*]

Enclosure: $15.00 Savings Coupon

Action Plan

Which part of this chapter will be most useful to you?

_____

_____

_____

How will you use these ideas?

_____

_____

_____

On what date will you begin using the ideas?

_____

Acknowledgements

This book took two and a half years to write, but it is the result of 22 years of experience in sales and marketing and a lifetime of learning from interesting and talented people.

So, thanks to the following, for generously sharing ideas and knowledge.

The names you will see in this book: Ann Gaines, Patricia Fisher, Leslie Howe, Nancy Davis and Nordstrom Department Store—role model for excellent customer service. My appreciation to Michael LeBoeuf, Professor of Management at the University of New Orleans for one of the best quotes in this book. And special thanks to a very committed and focused sales professional: Linda Benson-Woods.

The names you will not see in this book: My son, Daniel, without whose help with computer software and hardware, I would still be using a typewriter. Thanks to Susan Neimes, publisher of *ENX Magazine*, for letting me practice on your readers, to Carl Cobb, editor of *RS&R News* for your patience and support and to Cate Weeks for editing and polishing my articles for *Recharger Magazine*.

And finally, my thanks go to Tom Chapman, my editor and inspiration—who reads every word I write, before anyone else sees it. He adds just the right touch and is indispensable when writer's block strikes.

Ann Barr

Printed in the United States
29482LVS00001B/280-288

9 781413 406757